Richmond

Graham Fruen

Student's BOOK

A2

Keep it REAL!

Contents

Starter

VOCABULARY Clothes

I can talk about clothes.

1 **Look at the pictures. What do you think Mia and Elliot's hobbies are? Read Mia's blog and check.**

2 S0.1 **Match the clothes to Mia and Elliot. Listen, check and repeat.**

boots coat hat jeans scarf shirt skirt socks T-shirt trainers

Mia: *boots, ...* **Elliot:** *...*

Mia's Fashion blog

About Blog Latest posts Search

Hi, I'm Mia. I'm fifteen years old and I'm from Newcastle. It's a big city in the north of England. I'm into fashion and photography. This is my favourite outfit. I've got a twin brother, Elliot. He's into skateboarding. There's a skate park at the end of our road, so you can usually find him there!

Mia

Elliot

3 **Work in pairs. How many more words for clothes can you think of?**

4 **When do people wear these things? Match the clothes with the places.**

1 shorts, sunglasses and a T-shirt
2 a uniform
3 a coat, a hat and a scarf
4 nice clothes and smart shoes
5 jeans, a jumper and trainers
6 shorts, trainers and a sports top

a to a friend's house
b to the park in winter
c to school
d to the beach in summer
e to a P.E. lesson
f to a wedding

5 **What are you wearing today? Make a list.**

a T-shirt, black jeans, ...

Family and friends

I can talk about family and friends.

6 S0.2 **Put the letters in the correct order to make words for family and friends. Listen, check and repeat.**

1 rnstaep 2 estris 3 trrobhe 4 lcnue
5 naut 6 sbet reidnf 7 msaclaest
8 nuocsi 9 nmdgara 10 drangda

7 **Copy and complete the table with words from Exercise 6. Can you add more words?**

Male	Female	Both

8 **Read the Look! box. Write the names of some of your friends and family in your notebook.**

Look! **Possessive 's and '**

We use 's and ' to show possession.
My best friend's name is Ethan.
My parents' names are Clare and Andrew.

GRAMMAR *be*: affirmative, negative and questions

I can ask and answer about personal information.

1 Read the grammar box. What are the affirmative, negative and question forms for *I*, *you*, *he/she/it*, *we* and *they*?

Affirmative: I'm, you're, he's, …

Affirmative	Negative
I'**m** from Newcastle.	She **isn't** from London.
Questions	**Short answers**
Are you into skateboarding?	Yes, I **am**. / No, I'**m not**.

2 S0.3 Copy and complete the interview with Elliot from page 4. Use the contracted form of *be* where possible. Listen and check.

What [1] … your name?

My name [2] … Elliot Wilson.

How old [3] … you?

I [4] … fifteen years old.

Who [5] … older – you or Mia?

Mia [6] … older than me – by ten minutes!

[7] … Mia in your class at school?

No, she [8] … . We [9] … in different classes.

[10] … your friends into skateboarding, too?

No, they [11] … . They [12] … mostly into football or video games.

3 Copy and complete the questions with the question words in the box.

How old   What   What time   When   Where   Who

1 … are you from?
2 … are you?
3 …'s your birthday?
4 …'s your favourite singer?
5 …'s your favourite film?
6 … is it now?

4 Work in pairs. Ask and answer the questions in Exercise 3. Think of more questions with the question words.

Where's your favourite place in the world?

There is / There are

I can use *There is / There are* to describe a place.

5 Copy and complete the grammar box with *is*, *isn't*, *are*, and *aren't*.

Affirmative

There [1] … / There'**s** a skate park in our road.
There [2] … some big houses.

Negative

There [3] … a cinema.
There [4] … any shops.

Questions	Short answers
[5] … there a basketball court?	Yes, there **is**. / No, there **isn't**.
[6] … there any restaurants?	Yes, there **are**. / No, there **aren't**.

6 Look at the picture of Mia and Elliot's grandparents. Complete the sentences with the correct form of *there is / there are*.

There's a comfortable sofa.
1 … some books on the shelves.
2 … a desk.
3 … an orange armchair.
4 … any lamps.
5 '… any plants?' 'Yes, … .'
6 '… a dog?' 'No, … , but … a cat!'

7 Write five or six sentences about your bedroom. Use the words in the box and your ideas.

bed   bookshelf   comics   desk   games console   headphones   lamps   mirrors   pictures   plants   wardrobe

There's a comfortable bed. There aren't any …

8 Work in pairs. Ask and answer about your bedrooms.

A: Is there a sofa in your bedroom?
B: No, there isn't. Are there any pictures in your bedroom?

FAST FINISHER

Describe your classroom. Use *there is* and *there are*.

There are 25 chairs. There's a …

VOCABULARY Activities

I can talk about activities.

1 S0.4 **Complete the survey with the verbs in the box. Listen, check and repeat.**

cook dance do drive make play read ride run speak swim write

The BIG Survey

Today's questions are:
What things can you do? What things can't you do?

I can [1] … a bike, but I can't [2] … a car.
Rob, 28

I can't [7] … – I don't like water. But I can [8] … five kilometres!
Judith, 65

I can [3] … the guitar, but I can't [4] … music. I play 'by ear'.
Anna, 17

I can [9] … in French but I can't [10] … it – I'm too shy!
Lucy, 19

I can't [5] … a meal, but I can [6] … a sandwich!
Tali, 15

I can [11] … , but I can't [12] … gymnastics.
Danny, 15

2 **Complete the mind maps with the verbs from Exercise 1. Add an extra word to each mind map.**

School subjects

I can talk about school subjects.

3 S0.5 **Match the school subjects in the box with the pictures. Listen, check and repeat.**

Art Drama English French Geography History Maths Music P.E. Science

4 **Match the exam questions with a school subject. Work in pairs. Can you answer the questions?**

1. What are the two longest rivers in the world?
2. In which century and decade was World War I?
3. Which famous Spanish painter painted *The Old Guitarist*?
4. **Is a whale a fish, a mammal or a reptile?**
5. If a car is travelling at 90 km per hour, how long will it take to travel 270 km?

GRAMMAR *can* and *can't*

I can talk about ability.

1 **Read the grammar box. Choose the correct word to complete the rule.**

Affirmative	Negative
I **can** play the guitar.	She **can't** swim.
Questions	**Short answers**
Can you ride a horse?	Yes, I **can**. / No, I **can't**.

Rule

After *can* and *can't*, we use a verb [1]*with* / *without* **to**.

2 **PRONUNCIATION** *can* and *can't*

S0.6 **Listen and repeat.**

/ə/	/æ/	/ɑː/
Can you swim?	Yes, I **can**.	No, I **can't**.

3 S0.7 **Listen and repeat.**

'Can you speak German?' 'Yes, I can.'
'Can you drive a car?' 'No, I can't.'

4 **Write true sentences about you with *can* or *can't*.**

1 I / run / five kilometres.
2 I / say / 'hello' and 'goodbye' in three languages.
3 I / name / four countries beginning with A.
4 I / make / a sandwich.
5 I / swim / the length of a pool underwater.
6 I / count / backwards from twenty in English.

5 **Work in pairs. Ask and answer the questions from Exercise 4.**

A: Can you run five kilometres?
B: Yes, I can. Can you?

have got

I can use *have got* to talk about possessions and appearance.

6 **Copy and complete the grammar box. What are the full forms of *'ve* and *'s*?**

Affirmative	Negative
I**'ve got** a new bike. He**'s got** school today.	We **haven't got** a sister. She **hasn't got** a dog.
Questions	**Short answers**
Have you **got** a brother? [1]... he ... a new bike?	Yes, I **have**. / No, I **haven't**. Yes, he [2]... / No, he [3]... .

7 **Look at the picture. Copy and complete the sentences with the correct form of *have got*.**

Elsie *has got* long fair hair.
1 Alex and Ben ... white T-shirts.
2 Ben ... a hat.
3 Elsie and Ben ... glasses.
4 Elsie: 'I ... a mobile phone.'
5 Ben and Alex: 'We ... long hair!'
6 '... Ben and Alex ... phones?' 'No, they ... .'
7 '... Elsie ... long hair?' 'Yes, she ... .'

8 **Work in pairs. Ask and answer questions about your friends and family.**

A: Has your sister got a guitar?
B: Yes, she has.

Have Has	you your best friend your brother your sister your parents	got	long / short / brown hair? blue / green / brown eyes? a bike / a car / a motorbike? a cat / a dog / a pet? a laptop / a games console? a guitar / a violin?

FAST FINISHER

Describe your favourite celebrities. Use *have got*.

Dua Lipa has got dark hair and brown eyes.

READING

I can understand different forms of grammar in a text.

1 S0.8 **Read and listen to Kieran's blog and answer the questions.**

1 Where is Kieran from?
2 What does he say about his family?
3 What are his hobbies?

Hi, my name's Kieran. I'm fourteen years old and I'm from Newcastle. I go to a big secondary school in the north of the city. [1] ... more than 2,000 students. I really like my school. [2] ... a great gym where we can [3] ... basketball, and the teachers are all really nice. My favourite subjects [4] ... English and Geography.

I live near my school, so I can walk to school in the mornings. [5] ... a big park near my house, but there [6] ... many shops or restaurants – it's a quiet area. I've got an older brother. [7] ... name's Anand and he's sixteen. I've also got a younger sister. [8] ... name's Meera and she's eleven. We're all quite tall, and we've got dark hair and brown eyes – the same as [9] ... parents.

[10] ... do I do in my free time? I like all types of sport, especially football and Formula 1 racing. In my bedroom, I've got lots of posters of my favourite sports stars. I also love music, but only to listen to. I can't play an instrument and I've got a terrible singing voice!

2 Choose the correct answer to complete the blog.

1 a There's b There are c They are
2 a It's got b He's got c She's got
3 a to play b play c playing
4 a am b is c are
5 a There's b There are c It's got
6 a not b isn't c aren't
7 a Your b Her c His
8 a Your b Her c His
9 a us b our c we
10 a Who b Why c What

SPEAKING Introductions

I can introduce myself.

3 S0.9 **Listen and read. What three things have Kay and Charlie got in common?**

Kay: Hi, are you new here?
Charlie: Yes, I am. It's my first day.
Kay: Mo, too! My name's Kay. What's your name?
Charlie: I'm Charlie. Nice to meet you, Kay. So, what year are you in?
Kay: I'm in Year 9.
Charlie: So am I! I'm in Mrs Ryan's class. She's really nice. Whose class are you in?
Kay: I've got Mr Bliss. He's OK, but he's quite strict.
Charlie: What's your favourite subject?
Kay: Probably Maths, but I like History, too.
Charlie: Hmm, I'm not keen on Maths, but I like History.
Kay: Oh, there's the bell – time to go. I can't be late for Mr Bliss! See you later.
Charlie: Yes, see you around.

4 S0.10 **Listen and repeat the Useful language.**

Useful language

Introductions

Are you new here?
What's your name?
Nice to meet you.
What year are you in?
Whose class are you in?
What's your favourite subject?

5 Here are some more questions to ask a new student. Put the words in the correct order.

1 old / how / you / are / ?
2 brothers / you / any / got / or sisters / have / ?
3 do / live / where / you / ?
4 music / what type / of / like / do / you / ?
5 favourite / your / singer / is / who / ?

6 Work in pairs. Imagine you're at a new school. Write a new dialogue. Use the Useful language and the questions in Exercise 3. Then practise your dialogue.

FAST FINISHER

Think of other questions to ask a new student at school.

Are you in any after-school clubs?

On screen 1

Vocabulary: Types of film; Adjectives to describe films | **Grammar:** Present simple; Adverbs of frequency; Present continuous | **Speaking:** Making suggestions | **Writing:** A film review

VOCABULARY Types of film

I can talk about different types of film.

1 1.1 **Match the words in the box with the films in the online film store. Listen, check and repeat.**

action film   animated film   comedy   documentary   drama   fantasy film
historical film   horror film   musical   science-fiction film

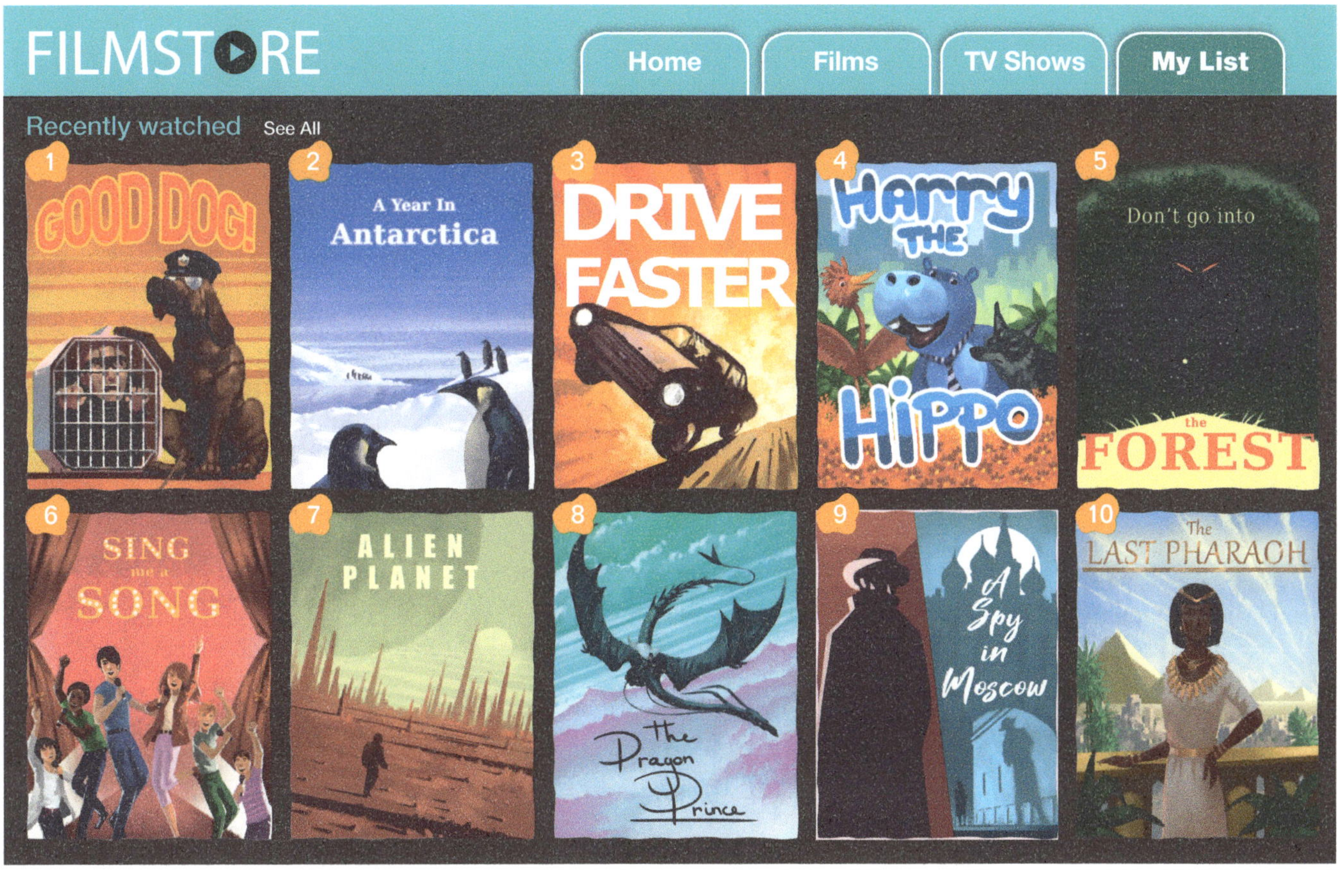

2 **Work in pairs. Think of examples of each type of film.**

The Incredibles is an animated film.

3 **Match the types of films with the descriptions.**

1 Don't watch this type of film on your own – it's scary!
2 There are lots of songs in this type of film.
3 This type of film doesn't use actors. It uses interviews with real people.
4 This type of film can be about the future, for example, space travel.
5 People laugh when they watch this type of film.
6 This type of film uses drawings of people or animals.

4 **In pairs, do the questionnaire.**

Film Questionnaire

1 What types of film do you like? Why?
2 Which don't you like? Why?
3 How many films do you watch every month?
4 Do you usually watch films at home or at the cinema?
5 What's your favourite film? Why?
6 Who's your favourite actor?

Now watch the vlog.

FAST FINISHER

Write about your partner's answers to the questionnaire.

Yolanda likes comedies and fantasy films. She ...

LS Language summary: Unit 1 SB p. 127

Films or books?

READING

I can understand different opinions in a forum.

1 1.2 **Read and listen to the forum. Copy the table and complete it with the names.**

Who prefers films?	
Who prefers books?	
Who likes films and books?	

YourOpinion.org — Home — Topics — New — Create Discussion — Log in

ARE FILMS BETTER THAN BOOKS?

Do you prefer watching films or reading books?
Click on the buttons and tell us what you think.
Are films better than books?

Yes or No

48% Say Yes — 52% Say No

Amy *posted 3 minutes ago*
My best friend doesn't agree, but I think films are more exciting. Science-fiction films often have amazing music and special effects – *Star Wars*, for example. You never get that with books.

Daniel *posted 12 minutes ago*
I like reading more than watching films because with books you get the whole story. Directors often cut the little details that make the book special, or sometimes they change the plot completely.

Karl *posted 26 minutes ago*
I think books are better because you can take them anywhere. I always read on the bus, for example. OK, you can do that with films on your phone, too, but the screen is really small, so it's harder to enjoy.

Melissa *posted 42 minutes ago*
I love reading and going to the movies. I usually read a book every two weeks and I go to the cinema with my friends at least once a month. Which do I like more? I can't choose, sorry!

Johnny *posted 1 hour ago*
It usually takes me a month to read a book, but I can watch a film in two hours! I love fantasy films such as *The Lord of the Rings*, but the books are really long and impossible to read.

Laura *posted 1 hour ago*
When I read a book, I like imagining what the people and places in the story look like. I'm often disappointed when I see the film. For example, in the *Percy Jackson* films, the characters aren't how I imagined at all.

2 Read the forum again and answer the questions. Who ...

1 says it's quicker to watch a film?
2 creates a picture of the characters in his/her head?
3 likes films with special effects?
4 often carries a book with him/her?
5 says that the story in a film is sometimes different from the book?
6 watches films with other people?

3 Word Power **Complete the sentences with the blue words from the forum.**

1 Hermione Granger and Ron Weasley are my favourite film ... .
2 I didn't understand that film. Can you explain the ... ?
3 Alfonso Cuarón is a Mexican film ... .
4 The ... in the new *Avengers* film are amazing.

4 Work in groups. Do you prefer watching films or reading books? Why? Compare your opinions.

5 FIND OUT **Who wrote *The Lord of the Rings*? How many books are there? How long did it take the author to write the first book?**

GRAMMAR Present simple

I can talk about facts, habits and routines.

Now watch the grammar animation.

1 **Read the grammar box. Copy and complete the rules with *regularly* and *true*.**

Affirmative

I/You/We/They often **go** to the cinema.
He/She **prefers** books to films.

Negative

I/We/You/They **don't talk** about books.
He/She **doesn't agree** with me.

Questions	Short answers
Do you **like** reading?	Yes, I **do**. / No, I **don't**.
Does he **read** on the bus?	Yes, he **does**. / No, he **doesn't**.

Rules

We use the present simple to talk about things that are [1] ... or that happen [2] ... .

2 **Complete the text with the correct form of the verb in brackets.**

Film directors often *make* (make) films from books. But sometimes they [1] ... (not follow) the original story! For example, in *The Hunger Games*, Peeta [2] ... (lose) a leg in the book, but in the film he [3] ... (not lose) it!

In one of the *Jurassic Park* films, some men [4] ... (take) a T-Rex and its baby to the USA. The T-Rex [5] ... (escape) and [6] ... (kill) a lot of people. This [7] ... (not happen) in the book – the dinosaurs [8] ... (not leave) the island!

3 **Write questions using the present simple.**

1 your town / have a cinema?
2 How often / you / go to the cinema?
3 Who / you / go with?
4 How much / a ticket / cost?
5 you / like horror films?

4 **Work in pairs. Ask and answer the questions from Exercise 3.**

A: Does your town have a cinema?
B: Yes, it does.

Adverbs and expressions of frequency

I can describe how often I do things.

5 **Read the grammar box and rules. Then read the posts in the forum on page 10 again and find more adverbs and expressions of frequency.**

I'm **often** disappointed.
Directors **sometimes** change the plot.
I go to the cinema **once a month**.
I read a book **every two weeks**.
You **never** get that with books.

Rules

Adverbs of frequency go after the verb *be*, but before other verbs.

We usually put expressions of frequency like *once a month/every two weeks* at the end of a sentence.

6 **Write true sentences about you. Include an adverb or expression of frequency.**

My friends and I watch action films.
My friends and I watch action films every Friday night.

1 I watch horror films in bed.
2 I buy a new book from a bookshop or online.
3 My parents let me download films from the internet.
4 We watch a film in English class.
5 I turn my phone off in the cinema.

7 **Work in pairs or small groups. Discuss your answers.**

A: I often watch horror films in bed.
B: Me, too.
C: Really? I never watch horror films in bed. They give me bad dreams!

8 **GET CREATIVE** **Write a questionnaire for your classmates, for example: *How often do you watch science-fiction films? Do you like horror films: a lot, not much, not at all?* Draw a chart to present the results.**

FUN FACT

In the famous Hollywood film *The Wizard of Oz*, Dorothy's magic shoes are red. The pair of shoes from the film is worth millions of dollars. But in the original book, the shoes were silver!

FAST FINISHER

Write a post for the forum on page 10. Give your opinion on the question: *Are films better than books?*

LS Language summary: Unit 1 SB p. 127

Be part of the action!

VOCABULARY and LISTENING Adjectives to describe films

I can listen for key words.

1 1.3 **Match the adjectives to describe films in the box with the icons. Listen, check and repeat.**

boring	brilliant	confusing	enjoyable	exciting	funny	romantic	sad	scary	serious	silly	terrible

2 **Choose the correct adjective.**

1 I don't like horror films. They're too *scary / terrible / enjoyable*.
2 The film was *brilliant / confusing / sad*. I didn't understand it.
3 The scene where Mufasa dies in *The Lion King* is very *sad / funny / enjoyable*.
4 It was *an enjoyable / an exciting / a terrible* film. I give it 1 out of 10.
5 Jack and Rose's first kiss in *Titanic* was very *confusing / romantic / scary*.
6 The film was *silly / funny / boring*. I fell asleep after twenty minutes!
7 The actors were very *boring / funny / sad*. We laughed and laughed!
8 We watched a *serious / funny / romantic* documentary about plastic pollution.

3 **Ask and answer about films that you watched recently.**

A: What do you think of the new Star Wars *film?*
B: The special effects are exciting, but the plot is confusing.

4 **Read the advert. What do you think a 4D cinema is? What happens in a 4D cinema that doesn't happen in a normal cinema?**

5 1.4 **Listen to the radio programme. Which of the experiences in the advert does Adam mention? What does he think about his first time in a 4D cinema?**

6 1.4 **Listen again and answer the questions.**

1 Where is James Bond when Adam's seat first starts moving?
2 What happens to his seat when the cars are driving fast?
3 Where is Bond when it starts snowing?
4 Why does Adam say, 'Luckily, I'm wearing a coat'?
5 What is the weather like in Brazil?
6 What can Adam smell?

7 **THINK CRITICALLY** **Why do you think going to the cinema is such a popular thing to do? Why do some people prefer to watch films at home?**

LS Language summary: Unit 1 SB p. 127

GRAMMAR Present continuous

I can talk about actions in progress now.

Now watch the grammar animation.

1 **Copy and complete the grammar box with the correct forms of the verb *be*.**

Affirmative

I [1] ... **wearing** a coat.
He/She**'s driving** through Rome.
You/We/They [2] ... **relaxing**.

Negative

I**'m not sitting** on a beach.
He/She [3] ... **moving**.
You/We/They **aren't talking**.

Questions	Short answers
Am I **going** fast?	Yes, I **am**. / No, I [4] ... .
Is it **following** us?	Yes, it [5] ... . / No, it **isn't**.
Are they **skiing**?	Yes, they **are**. / No, they [6] ... .

2 **Look at the picture from the film *Mission: Impossible – Fallout*. Complete the description with the correct present continuous form of the verb in brackets.**

Ethan Hunt (Tom Cruise) [1] … (ride) a motorbike through Paris. A lot of police officers [2] … (follow) him. Three of them [3] … (ride) motorbikes and the others [4] … (drive) cars. They [5] … (go) really fast, but they [6] … (not go) as fast as Ethan. Ethan [7] … (wear) a black leather jacket, but he [8] … (not wear) a helmet. What [9] … the other people in his team [10] … (do)? They [11] … (wait) for him in a boat. Come on, Ethan!

3 **Write questions using the present continuous. Ask and answer them in pairs.**

1 What / you / wear / today?
2 your teacher / use / a computer?
3 it / rain / outside?
4 What / your parents / do / today?
5 What / you / study / in history?
6 you / watch / a good TV series / at the moment?

4 PRONUNCIATION Contractions

1.5 **Listen and repeat.**

Full form	Contraction
I am driving.	I'm driving.
She is sitting.	She's sitting.
You are watching.	You're watching.
We are reading.	We're reading.
They are cooking.	They're cooking.

5 1.6 **Listen and write the sentences in your notebook.**

Present simple and present continuous

I can use the present simple and present continuous correctly.

6 **Read the grammar box. Choose the correct answers to complete the rules.**

Present simple	Present continuous
I often **ride** my bike to school.	He**'s riding** a motorbike through Paris.
It usually **snows** in winter.	It**'s snowing** in the film.

Rules

We use the present [1] *continuous / simple* to talk about facts, habits and routines.

We use the present [2] *continuous / simple* to talk about actions in progress now.

7 1.7 **Complete the phone conversation. Listen and check.**

Ivan: Hi, Anna. What [1] ... (you / do) at the moment?
Anna: It's movie night! I [2] ... (watch) a film with my family.
Ivan: [3] ... (you / always / watch) a film together on Friday night?
Anna: Yes, we do! My dad [4] ... (download) a new film every week. Then we [5] ... (turn off) the lights and imagine that we're in the cinema!
Ivan: That's a great idea. [6] ... (you / usually / have) popcorn, too?
Anna: Yes – my brother [7] ... (make) some in the kitchen now!
Ivan: Lucky you!
Anna: What about you? What [8] ... (you / do)?
Ivan: I'm at Pat's house. We [9] ... (play) video games and [10] ... (listen) to music.
Anna: Have fun!
Ivan: You, too! Bye!

FAST FINISHER

Choose a picture in Unit 1. Describe what is happening in the picture.

LS Language summary: Unit 1 SB p. 127

KEEP TALKING!

It sounds scary!

READING and LISTENING

I can find information in an events guide.

About | Latest news | What's on | Events

WHAT'S ON

Our top tips for events in your area

Saturday, 13 October

The Dark Forest (12+)

A group of teenagers spend the night in the forest. But they aren't alone ...

ABC Cinema 3 p.m.

Tickets: £9 Under 16s: £7

BUY TICKETS

Crazy Creatures

Fun animated film for all the family. With the voices of John Rodriguez and Margot Jackson.

Odeon Cinema 3.15 p.m.

Tickets: £8 Under 16s: £6.50

BUY TICKETS

Mad about Manga

Explore the history of manga, and dress as your favourite manga character!

Modern Art Gallery

Free

RESERVE

Dinosaur World

They walk. They roar. Don't miss this exhibition of life-size moving dinosaurs!

Victoria Museum

£10 Under 16s: Half price

BUY TICKETS

Safari in the City

For one day only, enjoy a very special tour of the zoo with TV presenter, Holly Bruce.

City Zoo 10 a.m. and 2 p.m.

Tickets: £15

SOLD OUT

Karate Class

Do you want to learn karate? All of our classes are free this week, so come and try it!

Sports Centre 3 p.m. and 5 p.m. Monday – Saturday

Free

RESERVE

1 **Look at the events guide. Do you know any web pages like this for your town or area?**

2 **Read the events guide and find answers to these questions.**

1 How old must you be to see *The Dark Forest*?
2 What type of film is *Crazy Creatures*?
3 Which events don't cost any money?
4 How much is a child's ticket for Dinosaur World?
5 At which event can you dress up in special clothes?
6 Where can you meet a famous person?
7 What time does the afternoon tour of the zoo start?
8 How many free karate classes are there?

3 1.8 **Listen. Which events from the web page do you hear?**

4 1.8 **Listen again and answer the questions.**

1 Which colour belts is the karate class for?
2 What does *yame* mean?
3 Where is the noise coming from in *The Dark Forest*?
4 Who goes to investigate the noise?
5 Where does the snake in the zoo come from?
6 How long is the snake?

SPEAKING Making and responding to suggestions

I can make and respond to suggestions.

1 1.9 **Listen and read. Which of the events on page 14 do Alex and Meera decide to go to?**

Alex: What shall we do this afternoon?
Meera: How about going to the cinema? There's a new horror film.
Alex: *The Dark Forest*? That sounds scary. I'm not sure. I'd prefer to see *Crazy Creatures*.
Meera: Hmm, I don't really like animated films.
Alex: Why don't we go to the zoo, then? There's a safari day.
Meera: OK, that's fine by me.
Alex: Oh, it's sold out already. What about going to the art gallery? There's a manga exhibition, and it's free.
Meera: Great idea! I love manga.
Alex: OK, let's go!

2 1.10 **Listen and repeat the Useful language.**

Useful language

Making suggestions

What shall we do this afternoon/tomorrow?
How about / What about ...?
Why don't we ...?

Responding

I'm not sure.
That sounds scary/boring/exciting.
I'd prefer to ...
That's fine by me.

3 1.11 **Copy and complete the dialogue with the words in the box. Listen and check.**

about don't exciting going shall to go

Ana: What [1] ... we do tomorrow?
Milo: How about [2] ... for a bike ride?
Ana: I'm not sure. I'd prefer [3] ... to a theme park.
Milo: Hmm, that sounds expensive. And I don't really like theme parks. What [4] ... going fishing?
Ana: That doesn't sound very [5] ... !
Milo: OK. Why [6] ... we go to the beach? We can go swimming and then have lunch there.
Ana: Great idea!

4 **Work in pairs. Make suggestions for what to do tomorrow and make a plan. Follow the steps in the Speaking plan.**

Speaking plan

Prepare

- Choose some of the events from page 14, or think of your own.
- Make notes for your dialogue.

Speak

- Practise your dialogue.
- Use phrases from the **Useful language** box.
- Act out your dialogue without notes.

Reflect

- How can you improve next time?
- Swap roles and choose new events.

Now play *Keep moving!*

FAST FINISHER

Write your own events guide like the one on page 14. Include two or three events or activities in your area.

EXPLORE CULTURE!

Great British animation

I can compare famous animated characters in the UK with animated characters in my country.

The World of Wallace and Gromit

Aardman Animations is a British animation company. Its two most famous animated characters are Wallace and Gromit. Wallace is an inventor who invents crazy things, and Gromit is his dog and best friend. Together they have lots of exciting and very funny adventures, but they always find time for a cup of tea!

Aardman's style of animation is unusual. These days, most animation companies use computers to create their characters, but Aardman uses models. So, how exactly do they do it?

First, the animators build a model of the character out of clay. Then, they take a picture of the character with a special camera. Next, the animators move parts of the character, for example, its eyes, its mouth or its fingers, and they take another picture. Finally, they put the pictures together to make a film, and the characters appear to move!

The work is very slow. They take 24 pictures for every second of film, and in a typical day, they create just two to three seconds of film! It can take two years to make a complete film. It's a lot of hard work, but the results are amazing.

The Aardman team have won lots of awards, including several Oscars. Their films are very popular with British people of all ages, and it's a Christmas tradition to watch Wallace and Gromit on TV! People love them because they live an ordinary British life: they drink tea, they like toast and jam, and they live in a typical British house. And people love the funny and imaginative stories, and the incredible animation.

1 Look at the pictures on page 16. Do you know these animated characters? What do you know about them?

2 1.12 Read and listen to the article. Find three reasons why Wallace and Gromit are popular.

3 Read the article again. Find and correct five more mistakes in the summary below.

~~American~~ ✗ *British* ✓

Aardman Animations is an American animation company. The company uses computers to create the characters. It's a very slow way to work. It takes one year to make a film. Wallace and Gromit are two of Aardman's most famous characters. Wallace is a taxi driver and Gromit is a dog. They love coffee and toast and jam. British people enjoy watching the films at Easter.

4 **Word Power** We use words like *first* and *then* to show the order of events. Find two more words in the text that show the order of events.

5 Work in pairs. Close your books. Explain to your partner how they make films at Aardman Animations. Then swap roles.

First, ... *Then, ...* *Next, ...* *Finally, ...*

6 1.13 Work in pairs. Read *How to make a cup of tea ... with Wallace and Gromit!* Put the instructions in the correct order. Then listen and check.

7 **COMPARE CULTURES** Which cartoons and other animated films and TV shows are popular in your country? Who are your favourite characters? What do you like about them?

Now watch the culture video.

FAST FINISHER

Describe your favourite character in a cartoon or animated film.

One of my favourite characters is SpongeBob SquarePants. He lives underwater in a pineapple.

How to make a cup of tea ... with Wallace and Gromit!

You will need ...

a kettle

water

a teabag

a cup

milk

sugar

Instructions

a. Take the teabag out of the water.

b. Enjoy!

c. Next, add the hot water.

d. First, boil some water in a kettle.

e. Finally, add some milk (and sugar, if you like).

f. Leave the teabag in the water for one or two minutes.

g. Then, put a teabag in a cup.

My favourite film

WRITING A film review

I can write a film review.

1 **Look at the picture. Do you know this film? Discuss in pairs what happens, or what you think happens, in the film.**

2 **Read the film review. What does the reviewer think of the actors in the film?**

The Martian

A film review

One of my favourite films is *The Martian*. It's a science-fiction film. I watched it on TV last month and I really enjoyed it.

The film is set in the future. A team of scientists are living and working on Mars. One day, there is a storm. A large piece of metal hits one of the astronauts, Mark Watney, and the other scientists think that he's dead. They decide to leave the planet and return to Earth. However, Mark isn't dead, and when he wakes up, he is alone on Mars. He now needs to find a way to survive and to contact Earth ...

The film is really enjoyable. The actors are excellent, especially Matt Damon as Mark Watney. The plot is simple, but the special effects are amazing and the music is great. The film is quite funny in parts, and the ending is very exciting! In conclusion, I totally recommend it.

by Louise Wilcox

3 **Look at the Useful language. How do you say these expressions in your language?**

Useful language

Reviewing a film

One of my favourite films is ...	The special effects are ...
The film is set in ...	The plot is simple/confusing.
The actors are ...	The ending is exciting/silly.

4 **Read the Look! box. Then look at the end of the review. What type of punctuation do we use after *In conclusion*?**

Look! Writing a conclusion

We often finish a film review with a conclusion: one or more sentences where you give your final opinion about the film. We can use *In conclusion* to introduce our final opinion.

5 **Match sentences 1–4 and a–e. Use them to write conclusions in your notebook. Include *In conclusion*.**

The plot is confusing and the actors are really bad.

The plot is confusing and the actors are really bad. In conclusion, it's a terrible film.

1 The actors are great and the songs are brilliant.
2 It's really scary and the ending is very imaginative.
3 The actors are good, but the story is boring.
4 It's a love story, but it's also very funny.

a if you like horror films, this is for you.
b I really enjoyed this musical.
c it's a great romantic comedy.
d ~~it's a terrible film.~~
e there are good things and bad things about this film.

6 **Write a film review. Follow the steps in the Writing plan.**

Writing plan

Prepare

- Choose one of your favourite films.
- Make notes about the plot.
- Think about your opinions of the actors, special effects, ending, etc.

Write

- Organize your ideas into paragraphs:
  - The name of the film and when you saw it
  - A short summary of the plot
  - Your conclusion
- Use the expressions from the **Useful language** box.

Check

- Check your grammar: present simple and present continuous.
- Check your spelling.

W **Writing summary** WB p. 84 E **Exams: Unit 1** SB p. 118 L **Language summary: Unit 1** SB p. 127

Good job!

2

Vocabulary: Jobs around the home; Jobs | **Grammar:** Past simple; *be*: past simple; *could* and *couldn't* | **Speaking:** Talking about skills and abilities | **Writing:** A biography

VOCABULARY Jobs around the home

I can talk about jobs around the home.

1 2.1 **Complete the survey with the expressions in the box. Use the *-ing* form of the verb. Listen and check.**

1 a tidying your room

clean the bathroom   do the laundry   do the shopping   do the washing up   lay the table   load the dishwasher   make dinner   make your bed   take out the rubbish/recycling   tidy your room   wash the car   wash the floor

JOBS AROUND THE HOME

Do you help at home? Here are the results of our survey of British teenagers.

1 Which jobs do you do most often?

88% of you do chores, and the ones you do most often are:

a

b
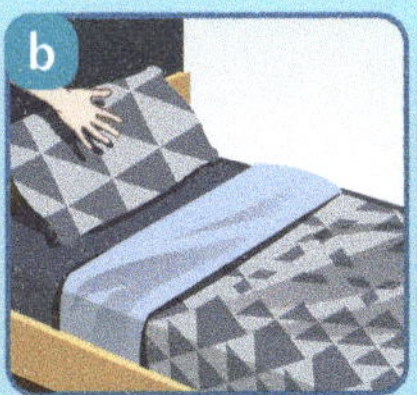

c

2 Which jobs do you complain about the most?

90% of you complain about doing chores! The three most hated jobs are:

d

e

f

3 Which are your favourite jobs?

63% of you are happy to help cook! These are your two favourite jobs:

g

h

4 Which jobs do you never do?

Most of you never help with these jobs:

i

j

5 Which jobs do your parents pay you to do?

Parents pay **47%** of you for doing jobs. These are the jobs that parents most often pay for:

k

l

2 **Read the survey. Which results surprise you? Which results don't surprise you?**

3 **Which jobs do you help with? Write sentences with *often, sometimes, hardly ever* and *never*.**

I often take out the rubbish.

4 **Ask and answer the questions in pairs.**

1 Which jobs do you hate doing?
2 Which jobs don't you mind doing?
3 Which jobs are easy?
4 Do you sometimes argue with your parents about jobs around the home? When and why?

5 **THINK CRITICALLY** **Discuss in pairs. Is it important for children and teenagers to do jobs around the home? Why/Why not?**

Now watch the vlog.

FAST FINISHER

Make a list of more jobs around the home. How many can you think of?

tidy the living room, walk the dog, ...

LS Language summary: Unit 2 SB p. 128

Amazing inventions

READING

I can understand the main idea of a text.

1 2.2 **Read and listen to the article. What is the 'Boot Buddy'? What job does it help with? Is it successful?**

THE BOOT BUDDY

Like many teenagers, Arminder Dhillon from London didn't like doing the washing up or tidying his room, but the job he hated most was cleaning his muddy football boots. There wasn't an easy way to clean them after practice, and his mum complained when he brought mud into the house. Then one day, Arminder had an idea. He found a water bottle, a plastic knife and a small brush, and he put them together. When he started cleaning his boots, his older brother laughed. 'What are you doing?' he asked. 'Go and do it the normal way in the sink.' But to his brother's surprise, Arminder's idea worked!

Arminder didn't stop there. He made some drawings of his invention, and experimented with different designs. He then used a 3D printer to create a model. However, to start a business, Arminder needed money. He decided to appear on *Dragons' Den*, a television programme where people show their business ideas to a group of experts and millionaires, and ask for money to help them. Fifteen-year-old Arminder was very nervous when he stood up in front of the 'Dragons', but he knew this was his big opportunity. Did the Dragons like the idea? Yes, they did! Three of them agreed to give Arminder £20,000 each. He became the youngest person ever to succeed on the programme.

With the Dragons' help, Arminder now sells his invention, the 'Boot Buddy', all over the world. For footballers everywhere, it's an end to the problem of muddy boots!

2 Complete the sentences with the names of the people in the box.

Arminder (x3) footballers his brother his mum the Dragons

1 ... didn't like cleaning his football boots.
2 ... didn't want mud in the house.
3 ... created a new invention to make cleaning easier.
4 ... thought that Arminder's invention was silly.
5 ... went on a TV show with his invention.
6 ... helped Arminder with his business.
7 ... use the 'Boot Buddy'.

3 Word Power **Read the definition of a compound noun. Make five more compound nouns with the words in the boxes.**

compound noun
two nouns together which make one new noun, for example, *football boots*

boxing golf ice swimming tennis

ball costume gloves racket skates

4 GET CREATIVE **Work in pairs or small groups. Think of a job around the home that you don't like doing. Invent some ideas to make the job easier. Present your ideas to the class.**

5 FIND OUT **What machines did these people invent to help with household chores?**

1 William Henry Hoover
2 Alva John Fisher

GRAMMAR Past simple

I can talk about events in the past.

Now watch the grammar animation.

1 Read the grammar box. Choose the correct answers to complete the rules.

Affirmative

Arminder **hated** cleaning his boots.
His older brother **laughed**.

Negative

He **didn't like** doing the washing up.
Arminder **didn't stop** there.

Questions	Short answers
Did the Dragons **like** Arminder's idea?	Yes, they **did**. / No, they **didn't**.

Rules

We form [1] *irregular / regular* verbs in the past simple by adding *-ed*.

To make negative sentences, we use [2] *did / didn't* + infinitive.

To make questions, we use [3] *didn't / did* + subject + infinitive.

2 Find the past simple form of these verbs in the article on page 20. Which verbs are regular?

become bring complain decide find
know make put stand start

3 Complete the text with the past simple affirmative of the verbs in brackets. Use the Irregular verbs list on page 136 to help you.

GREAT INVENTIONS: THE DISHWASHER

Josephine Cochrane *invented* (invent) the first dishwasher in the 1870s. She [1] … (live) in a big house and [2] … (have) a lot of dinner parties. Her servants always [3] … (do) the washing up, but one evening they [4] … (break) some of her expensive plates. That [5] … (give) Josephine an idea: why not invent a machine to wash the dishes? Josephine [6] … (draw) some designs, and then she [7] … (build) a model. In 1886, she [8] … (take) her dishwasher to an exhibition and she [9] … (win) a prize for the best invention. Now millions of homes around the world have a dishwasher!

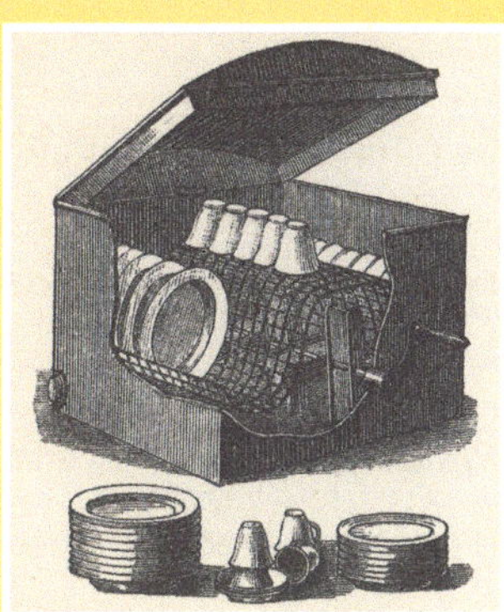

4 Lucy's parents are away for the weekend. Her messages to them aren't true. Correct the messages in your notebook.

I did my homework on Friday night. (go to a party)
She didn't do her homework on Friday night. She went to a party.

1 I got up early on Saturday. (stay in bed until 11.30)
2 After breakfast, I tidied my room. (watch TV)
3 Then I did the laundry. (meet her friends in town)
4 I cooked pasta for dinner. (order a pizza)
5 I cleaned the kitchen. (fall asleep)

5 PRONUNCIATION *-ed* endings

2.3 Listen and repeat.

/t/	/d/	/ɪd/
laughed	complained	decided

6 2.4 Listen and repeat the verbs you hear. Add them to the table.

7 Write questions in the past simple.

you / watch / any good films last night?
Did you watch any good films last night?

1 What / you / do / last weekend?
2 your dad / make / dinner yesterday?
3 you / lay / the table before dinner?
4 Where / you / go / on holiday in the summer?
5 What / you / do / there?

8 In pairs, ask and answer the questions in Exercise 7. Give more information if you can.

A: Did you watch any good films last night?
B: Yes, I did. I watched Captain Marvel.

FUN FACT

In 1963, an artist, Harvey Ball, drew a yellow smiling face for a local business. He received $45 for his design. Today, the 'smiley face' appears on T-shirts, bags, notebooks and more, and is worth $500 million a year.

FAST FINISHER

Write sentences about famous people and their creations. Use the verbs *invent, paint, write, sing*.

Leonardo da Vinci painted the 'Mona Lisa'. Ed Sheeran and Beyoncé sang 'Perfect'.

LS Language summary: Unit 2 SB p. 128

Before they were famous

VOCABULARY and LISTENING Jobs

I can listen for specific details in a podcast.

1 2.5 **Match the pictures with the jobs. Listen, check and repeat. In pairs, think of more jobs.**

dentist designer engineer farmer journalist lawyer mechanic
nurse personal trainer police officer receptionist shop assistant

1 
2 
3 
4 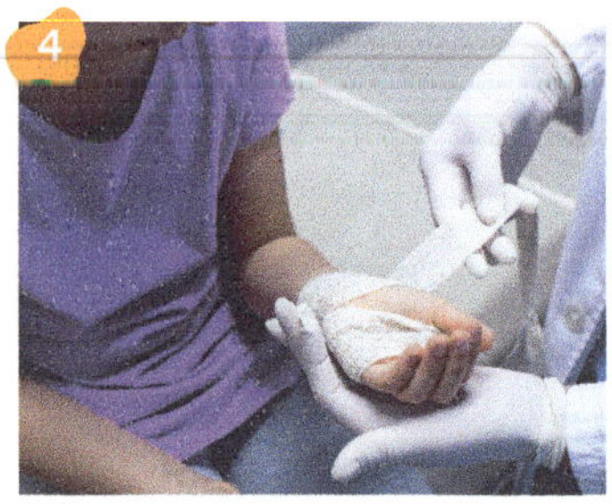
5 
6 
7 
8 

What's my job?

9 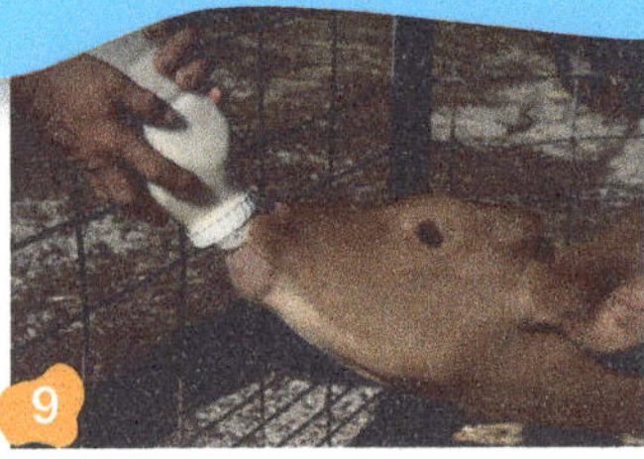
10 
11 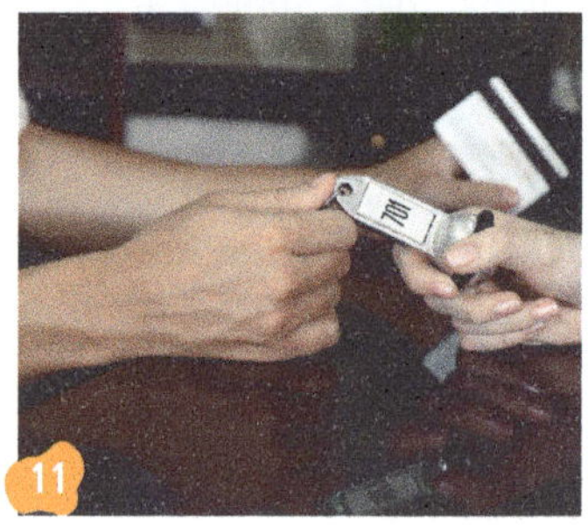
12 

2 Match six of the jobs in Exercise 1 with the descriptions. Who ...

1 looks after ill people?
2 builds bridges and roads?
3 repairs cars?
4 works in a gym and helps people to become fitter?
5 grows food and looks after animals?
6 writes news stories?

3 In pairs, think of more jobs. Ask and answer the questions.

1 Which jobs do you think are the most interesting?
2 Which jobs do you think are the hardest?
3 Which job would you like to do when you're older?

4 2.6 **Look at the pictures. What job(s) do these people do? Listen to the podcast. What jobs did they do before they were famous?**

5 2.6 **Copy the notes. Listen again and complete them.**

Before they were famous: Part One

Emma Stone worked in a [1] ... shop for [2] ... .

Hugh Jackman taught [3] ... and [4] ... when he was only [5] ... years old.

Lady Gaga's customers liked her because she was [6] ... .

LS Language summary: Unit 2 SB p. 128

GRAMMAR *be*: past simple

I can use *was* and *were* to talk about the past.

Now watch the grammar animation.

1 **Copy and complete the grammar box with *was*, *wasn't*, *were* and *weren't*.**

Affirmative

Her first job **was** in a cake shop.
His students [1] ... almost the same age.

Negative

It [2] ... an ordinary cake shop.
Most famous people **weren't** born rich.

Questions	Short answers
[3] ... she a waitress?	Yes, she **was**. / No, she **wasn't**.
Were they teachers?	Yes, they **were**. / No, they [4] ... .

2 2.7 **Copy and complete the sentences with the correct form of *was* or *were*. Listen and check.**

BEFORE THEY WERE FAMOUS: Part Two

The runner Usain Bolt is the winner of eight Olympic Gold medals. But [1] ... he interested in running at school? No, he [2] ... . His favourite sports [3] ... cricket and football!

Taylor Swift's first job [4] ... on a farm. It [5] ... an ordinary farm – it [6] ... a Christmas tree farm! Taylor's job [7] ... to look for insects on the trees and take them off!

As teenagers, the actors Matt Damon and Ben Affleck [8] ... at the same school. [9] ... they in the same class? No, they [10] ... , but they [11] ... good friends!

3 **Read the Look! box. What is the negative form of *there was* and *there were*?**

Look! ***there was / there were***

The past simple of *there is / there are* is *there was / there were.*
There was *a party at school yesterday.*
There were *lots of people at the bus stop this morning.*
Was there *a storm last night? Yes,* ***there was****.*

4 **George had a bad day yesterday. Copy and complete the sentences with the correct form of *there was* and *there were*.**

1 ... any milk in the fridge for breakfast. ✗
2 ... any buses so he was late for school. ✗
3 ... a Maths test at school. ✓
4 ... any difficult questions? Yes, ... ✓
5 ... a storm on the way home. ✓

could and *couldn't*

I can talk about ability in the past.

5 **Read the grammar box. Do *could* and *couldn't* have a different form for *he*, *she*, and *it*?**

Affirmative

I/You/He/She/It/We/They **could** sing and act.

Negative

I/You/He/She/It/We/They **couldn't** swim.

Questions	Short answers
Could you play the piano when you were six?	Yes, I **could**. / No, I **couldn't**.

6 2.8 **Write sentences about the people when they were young. Use *could/couldn't* and *was/were*. Then listen and check.**

Mozart / play the piano / when he / three
Mozart could play the piano when he was three.

1 Picasso / draw really well / when he / a child
2 Serena Williams / play tennis / when she / four
3 When he / fifteen, Michael Jordan / not / get into his school basketball team!
4 When he / sixteen, the astronaut Neil Armstrong / fly a plane, but he / not / drive a car
5 Before she / famous, the author JK Rowling / not / afford a computer. She wrote most of *Harry Potter* using a pen and paper!

7 **Work in pairs. Ask and answer the questions. Choose different ages.**

A: Could you swim when you were three?
B: No, I couldn't.
A: What about when you were seven?
B: Yes, I could swim when I was seven.

swim	two
cook a meal	four
speak English	seven
ride a bike	eight
use a computer	...

FAST FINISHER

Imagine you are a superhero. Write sentences about your superpowers when you were younger.

When I was two, I could climb tall buildings.

LS Language summary: Unit 2 SB p. 128

KEEP TALKING!

When can you start?

READING and LISTENING

I can understand job adverts.

1 **Work in pairs. At what age can teenagers in your country get a part-time or holiday job? Do you know any teenagers with a job?**

2 **Read the job adverts and match them with the pictures.**

a

WANTED! BABYSITTER

- Do you like looking after children?
- Are you sixteen or older?

We're a family with two young children. We're looking for a babysitter to work one or two evenings a week, Monday to Friday.

Call Tom or Delia on 519 6203

Newspaper boys and girls

- Are you fourteen or older?
- Can you ride a bike?

We're looking for someone to deliver newspapers to homes in the area. Monday to Friday. Start time 7 a.m. You will finish in time to get to school.

Please ask at Morton Newsagent's.

b

Sports camp assistant

Do you love sport? Do you like working with children? Do you want to work this summer holiday?

Energize is the UK's favourite sports camp for children. We're looking for confident people to organize activities five days a week. You must be fifteen or older.

Call Dan on **029 2018 0132**

c

Dog walker

Hello! My name is Lola and I'm three years old. I can be a bit naughty, but I'm very friendly!

My owner is looking for someone to take me for walks, five days a week during July and August. One or two hours a day is all the exercise I need!

So if you love dogs, then call my owner, Sarah, on 07700 900784.

d

Café helper

We're a small, friendly café. We're looking for a hard-working person (age fourteen or older) to clean the kitchen and do the washing up.

Hours of work: Saturday 11 a.m.–3 p.m.

Good pay. Free lunch!

Ask at the Dream Bean Café.

e

3 **Read about the people below. Which is the best job for each person? Which person can't do any of these jobs? Why not?**

1. Josie is fifteen. She's the captain of her school volleyball team. She also plays football and does athletics. She's hard-working and is good with children.
2. Sam is fourteen. He wants a weekend job, but he can't work on Sunday afternoons. He doesn't mind what job he does.
3. Megan is sixteen. She wants some extra money for her holiday next summer. She'd like a job that she can do before school.
4. Charlie is thirteen. He'd like to work in the summer holidays, but he also wants to have time to see his friends. He likes sport, animals and playing video games.
5. Duane is fifteen. He's interested in food and he's great with children (he has three younger sisters!). He's free to work on Saturday evenings and all day on Sunday.
6. Lucy is seventeen. She's studying for exams, but would like to work some evenings after school. She enjoys working with children and animals.

4 2.9 **Lucy phones Delia to find out more about the babysitting job. Listen. Is Lucy interested in the job?**

5 2.9 **Listen again and complete Lucy's notes in your notebook.**

Job:	*Babysitter*
Age of children:	[1] *… and …*
Days:	[2] *… and …*
Time:	*From* [3] *… to …*
Pay:	[4] *… per hour*

SPEAKING Talking about skills and abilities

I can take part in a simple job interview.

1 2.10 **Josie is having an interview for a job as a sports camp assistant. Listen and read. Do you think she gets the job? Why/Why not?**

Dan: Good morning, I'm Dan. Nice to meet you.
Josie: Hello, I'm Josie. Nice to meet you, too.
Dan: So, why are you interested in working at a sports camp?
Josie: Well, I love playing sports. I do athletics, and I also play football and volleyball.
Dan: How well can you play volleyball?
Josie: Oh, I can play very well. I play for my school team.
Dan: That's great. Do you enjoy working with children?
Josie: Yes, I do. I sometimes babysit for other families in my street, so I'm good at organizing games. I know how to keep children busy!
Dan: Perfect. Well, thank you for talking to me. We can let you know about the job next week.
Josie: Fantastic! I look forward to hearing from you.

2 2.11 Listen and repeat the **Useful language**.

Useful language

Asking about skills and abilities

Why are you interested in ...?
How well can you ...?
Do you enjoy ...?

Talking about your skills and abilities

Quite well. / Very well. / Not very well.
I'm (not very) good at ...
I love/enjoy ...
I know how to ...

3 2.12 **Tom is having an interview for a job as a waiter. Put the interview in the correct order. Listen and check.**

a **Int:** That's great – our foreign customers love that! Are you good at carrying plates?
b **Tom:** I can speak Spanish quite well, and I know how to say 'hello' and 'goodbye' in a few other languages.
c **Int:** Perfect. Thank you for talking to me.
d **Tom:** I'm friendly and I enjoy working with people.
e **Int:** Can you speak any languages? A lot of tourists visit the restaurant.
f **Tom:** Yes, I am. I often help my parents with jobs at home.
g **Int:** Why are you interested in working as a waiter?

4 Work in pairs. Interview each other for a part-time or holiday job. Follow the steps in the **Speaking plan.**

Speaking plan

Prepare

- Decide on your roles.
- Choose one of the job adverts from page 24.
- Make notes for your dialogue.

Speak

- Practise your dialogue.
- Use phrases from the **Useful language** box.
- Act out your dialogue without notes.

Reflect

- How successful was your interview? Do you think that you got the job?
- Swap roles and choose a new job advert.

Now play *Keep moving!*

FAST FINISHER

Think of your dream holiday job. Write an advert for it.

LS Language summary: Unit 2 SB p. 128

REAL CULTURE!

A famous writer

I can understand a biography of a famous person.

AGATHA CHRISTIE

THE QUEEN OF CRIME

Agatha Christie was an English writer. She is the world's best-selling novelist, with sales of two billion books in more than 100 languages.

1 Agatha Christie was born in 1890. She could read from a young age, and she loved adventure stories and detective novels. She always had lots of ideas for her own stories.

2 In 1914, the First World War started and Agatha became a nurse. She worked in a hospital and helped injured soldiers. There she learned all about medicines and poisons. This was useful for her detective stories – a lot of her murderers used poison to kill their victims!

3 After the war, Agatha wrote her first novel about the fictional detective Hercule Poirot. He was a Belgian police officer with smart clothes and a large moustache, and he was very clever. He was one of Agatha's most popular characters.

4 Agatha loved travelling. In 1928, she travelled to Istanbul in Turkey on the famous Orient Express train. During her trip, she met Max, an archaeologist, and they got married in 1930. Their marriage was very happy and lasted until Agatha died in 1976.

5 The journey to Istanbul gave Agatha an idea for one of her best-known stories, *Murder on the Orient Express*. In the novel, Hercule Poirot is a passenger on the Orient Express. On the second night, there is a murder on the train. The victim is an American, and the murderer is somewhere on the train. Who is it, and can Poirot solve the mystery?

6 Today, Agatha Christie's stories are popular all over the world. With her unusual characters, her mysterious murders and her brilliant detectives, she really is the 'Queen of Crime'.

1 **Discuss the questions as a class.**

1 Do you like reading detective stories or watching detective programmes on TV?
2 Who is your favourite detective?
3 Why do you think people enjoy detective stories and TV programmes?

2 2.13 **Listen and read about Agatha Christie and put the events in the correct order.**

1 g

a She travelled to Turkey.
b She wrote her first novel.
c She learned to read.
d She died.
e She got a job as a nurse.
f There was a war.
g She was born in England.
h She married Max.

3 **Read the biography again and answer the questions.**

1 What type of stories did Agatha like when she was little?
2 How was her time as a nurse useful to her as a writer?
3 What did her detective, Hercule Poirot, look like?
4 Agatha's husband was called Max. What was his job?
5 How long were they married?
6 What happened in *Murder on the Orient Express*?

4 **Word Power** **Match the crime words in blue in the biography with the definitions.**

1 a police officer who investigates crimes
2 a person who kills another person
3 to find an answer to a problem
4 a crime where a person kills another person
5 a liquid that can kill someone
6 a person who dies or is injured as the result of a crime

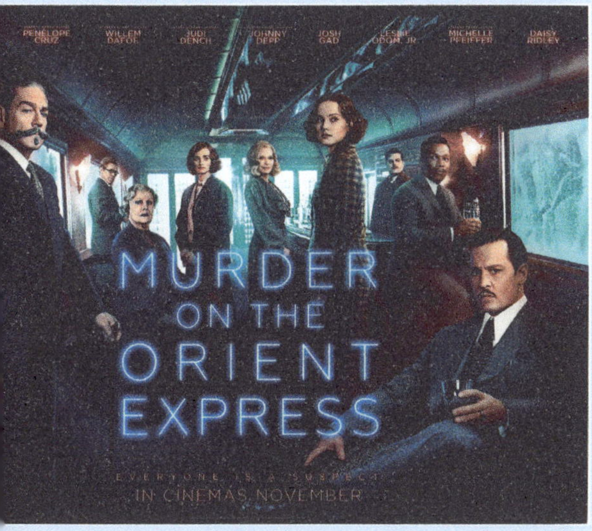

5 **Complete the article about a real mystery. Choose a, b or c.**

The mysterious disappearance of

AGATHA CHRISTIE

In 1926, Agatha Christie disappeared from her home in a real-life mystery. Where did she go and what happened?

At 9.30 p.m. on 3 December 1926, Agatha Christie got up from her armchair and walked upstairs. She said goodnight to her daughter and went back [1] … . She then got into her car and [2] … into the night. Nobody saw her for eleven days.

The police found her car about 25 km away. [3] … were some clothes in the car, but Agatha wasn't there. A week passed. A newspaper offered £100 for information. More [4] … a thousand police officers looked for her.

Then, after eleven days, a musician [5] … Agatha in a hotel 350 km away. She was safe and well. When Agatha's husband arrived to collect her, she [6] … remember anything.

What happened? We don't know. It's a mystery – just like one of her stories!

	a	b	c
1	downstairs	upstairs	outside
2	drive	drives	drove
3	They	There	It
4	than	that	what
5	looked	watched	saw
6	couldn't	can't	could

6 2.14 **Listen and check your answers.**

7 **COMPARE CULTURES** **Who are some of the most popular writers in your country? What type of books do they write?**

Now watch the culture video.

FAST FINISHER

Imagine you are a crime writer. Make notes about your next story. What was the crime? When and where did it take place? Who was the detective and how did he/she solve the crime?

An interesting life

WRITING A biography

I can write a biography.

1 **Read the biography of James Naismith. Why did he invent basketball?**

James Naismith: The inventor of BASKETBALL

James Naismith was a teacher, a sports coach and the inventor of basketball. He was born in 1861, in Canada, and he died in 1939.

James grew up on a farm and, as a child, he helped in the fields before and after school. From 1883 to 1887, he went to university in Montreal and studied P.E. He was a good athlete and loved all sports.

After university, James got a job as a P.E. teacher in the USA. For most of the year, his students played baseball, football and rugby, but winter was too cold for sport and the students got bored. James decided to invent an indoor sport. He put two fruit baskets on the walls of the gym and created a game that he called 'Basket Ball'.

'Basket Ball' quickly became popular all over the USA. In 1898, James became the first basketball coach at the University of Kansas, and he worked there until he retired. Today, more than 300 million people play basketball around the world.

Basketball then ...

... and now

2 **Look at the Useful language. How do you say these expressions in your language?**

Useful language

Writing about a person's life

He/She was born in ...
He/She died in ...
He/She grew up in/on ...
As a child, he/she ...
He/She went to university in ...
He/She got a job as a ...

3 **Read the Look! box. Which prepositions do we use to talk about ...**

1 the duration of an action in the past?
2 when an action ended?
3 when an action began and ended?

Look! **Prepositions of time**

We use prepositions of time to describe when something happened.
He studied P.E. ***from*** *1883* ***to*** *1887.*
His students played football ***for*** *most of the year.*
He worked there ***until*** *1937.*

4 **Complete the sentences with the correct preposition.**

1 My grandma was a pilot ... 1982 ... 2015.
2 My uncle worked in a factory ... eighteen years.
3 They lived in France ... 2015.
4 Her cousin was in hospital ... three weeks.
5 We waited for the bus ... ten o'clock.
6 Liam worked ... 9 a.m. ... 10 p.m.

5 **Write a biography of a famous person from the past. Follow the steps in the Writing plan.**

Writing plan

Prepare

› Choose a famous person you're interested in. Research and make notes about important events in his/her life.

Write

› Organize your ideas into paragraphs:
  - Introduction
  - Childhood
  - Career
  - Achievements
› Use the expressions from the **Useful language** box.

Check

› Check your grammar: past simple, *could*.
› Check prepositions of time and your spelling.

W Writing summary WB p. 85 E Exams: Unit 2 SB p. 119 L Language summary: Unit 2 SB p. 128

Survival stories

3

Vocabulary: Verbs of movement; Adjectives and adverbs | **Grammar:** Past continuous; Past simple; Past time expressions | **Speaking:** Telling a story and reacting | **Writing:** A narrative

VOCABULARY Verbs and prepositions of movement

I can describe different ways of moving.

Are you looking for a physical challenge?

Then the *Survivor Race* is for you! Our obstacle course will test you to the limit!

1 3.1 **Match the verbs in the box with the pictures. Listen, check and repeat.**

climb crawl dive fall jump pull push run swim walk

2 **Read the Look! box. Can you think of more prepositions of movement?**

> **Look! Prepositions of movement**
>
> We can use prepositions of movement after verbs to show how someone moves from one place to another.
>
> *We walked **through** the forest.*
>
> *She ran **up** the stairs.*

3 3.2 **Read the description of the obstacles in the *Survivor Race*. Choose the correct preposition. Listen and check.**

> **Our obstacle course**
>
> 1. Swim *across / up* the icy river!
> 2. Dive *over / into* the muddy lake!
> 3. Crawl *through / around* the tunnel!
> 4. Climb *along / over* the three-metre-high wall!
> 5. Pull a tyre *down / up* the hill!
> 6. Push the tyre *up / down* the hill!
> 7. Walk *along / into* the tree!
> 8. Don't fall *off / up*!
> 9. Run *across / around* the flag!
> 10. Finally, jump *onto / off* an air bag.
>
> Congratulations! You survived!

4 **GET CREATIVE** **Work in pairs. Design your own obstacle course and describe each obstacle. Use the verbs in Exercise 1 and the prepositions and nouns in Exercise 3.**

Crawl through the mud.

Now watch the vlog.

FAST FINISHER

Write sentences about last week using the verbs in Exercise 1. Remember to use the correct form of the past tenses.

I ran down the stairs at school. I climbed up a rope in P.E.

LS **Language summary: Unit 3** **SB** p. 129

An amazing rescue

READING

I can understand the sequence of events in a story.

TRAPPED!

In 2018, a boys' football team from Thailand survived for seventeen days in a cave. This is their amazing true story.

1 23 June

It was a Saturday afternoon. The boys from the Wild Boars football team were training as usual. One of the boys had a birthday that day, and the team was planning a celebration: a trip to a nearby cave.

After training, the boys cycled to the cave. They were laughing and joking as they climbed inside, but suddenly it started to rain. Soon the cave was filling with water. The boys tried to get out, but it was impossible. They were trapped ...

Back at home, the boys' parents were starting to worry. Where were the boys? They found their bikes near the cave, but there was no sign of the boys.

Inside the cave, the water was getting higher. The boys crawled further into the cave until finally they reached a flat rock, about four kilometres from the entrance. At last, they could stop and rest.

2 24 June

The next day, police officers and divers were at the cave, but it was still raining heavily. When the rescuers tried to enter, the water pushed them back. It was too dangerous to go in.

3 2 July

Eight days later, the boys were still missing. No one knew if they were alive or dead. Then, on Monday, 2 July, two divers were exploring a tunnel deep inside the cave when they heard voices. The boys were alive! But now they faced an even bigger challenge: how to get them out ...

To be continued ...

1 Look at the pictures from a true story. Do you know this story? What happened and where was it?

2 3.3 Read and listen to the story and check your ideas from Exercise 1.

3 Read the story again. Put the events in the correct order.

a The water got higher, so the boys crawled deeper into the cave.
b Finally, some divers found them.
c The parents found the boys' bikes.
d The weather changed.
e The rescuers couldn't reach the boys.
f The boys went to the cave.
g Football training ended.
h Police and divers arrived at the cave.

4 Word Power **We can often make a noun ending *-er* that means 'the person that does the action'. Copy and complete the table.**

verb	noun
begin	*beginner*
climb	*climber*
dive	1 ...
play	2 ...
rescue	3 ...
win	4 ...

5 THINK CRITICALLY **Imagine some friends are planning an exciting trip to a mountain, a desert, a cave, etc. What's your advice for a safe trip?**

6 FIND OUT **How many boys were in the cave?**

GRAMMAR Past continuous

I can talk about actions that were in progress in the past.

Now watch the grammar animation.

1 **Read the grammar box. Choose the correct answer to complete the rules.**

Affirmative

The cave **was** fill**ing** with water.
The boys **were** laugh**ing** and jok**ing**.

Negative

The water **wasn't** go**ing** down.
The boys **weren't** carry**ing** phones.

Questions	Short answers
Was it rain**ing**?	Yes, it **was**. / No, it **wasn't**.
Were the boys laugh**ing**?	Yes, they **were**. / No, they **weren't**.

Rules

We use the past continuous to talk about [1] *a long action in progress / a finished action* in the past.

We form the past continuous with the [2] *present / past* simple of *be* + *-ing* form.

2 3.4 **Complete the next part of the story with the past continuous affirmative. Listen and check.**

TRAPPED! Continued ...

2 July
The boys were alive! They were thin and hungry, but they [1] ... (do) well. Outside the cave, journalists [2] ... (report) the news. The whole world [3] ... (watch) and hoping.

3 July
The rescue team [4] ... (work) on a plan to get the boys out. It wasn't easy because the boys couldn't swim. Experts from all over the world [5] ... (help) with the rescue.

7 July
The divers [6] ... (get) ready to pull the boys out. A storm [7] ... (move) nearer and nearer, so they needed to work fast.

10 July
After seventeen days in the cave, all of the boys were finally out and safe! All around the world, people [8] ... (celebrate)!

3 **Write true sentences about you. Use the past continuous affirmative or negative.**

I / sit / on the bus at nine o'clock this morning.
I wasn't sitting on the bus at nine o'clock this morning.

1 I / do / my homework at eight o'clock last night.
2 We / learn / about electricity in Science last week.
3 It / rain / yesterday.
4 My parents / sleep / at 4.30 this morning.
5 My friends and I / text / each other / last night.

4 3.5 **Imagine there was a robbery at school last night. Complete the interview with the verbs in the box. Listen and check.**

do eat have play watch (x2)

Detective: What were you doing at eight o'clock last night?
Student: I [1] ... dinner.
Detective: What [2] ... you ... ?
Student: Pizza and salad.
Detective: Interesting. And what [3] ... you ... at nine o'clock?
Student: I [4] ... a film at my friend's house.
Detective: [5] ... your friend ... the film, too?
Student: No, he [6] ... a game on his phone.
Detective: Hmm, very suspicious.

5 **PRONUNCIATION** **Sentence stress**

3.6 **Listen and repeat. Copy the rhythm.**

A: What were you **doing** at **seven o'clock**?
B: I was **playing football**.
A: Who were you **playing** with?
B: I was **playing** with some **friends**.
A: Where were you **playing**?
B: We were **playing** at the **park**.

6 **Work in pairs: a detective and a student. Do your own interview about the robbery. Use the ideas below.**

Detective	Student
What ... at ...?	do my (Maths) homework
Who ... with?	do the washing up
Where ...?	listen to music
	sit (on a bus)
	tidy my room
	walk the dog
	your ideas

FAST FINISHER

What were you doing at these times yesterday? Write true sentences.

6 a.m. 8 a.m. 11.30 a.m. 5 p.m. 9 p.m.

LS Language summary: Unit 3 SB p. 129

Jungle survival

VOCABULARY and LISTENING Adjectives and adverbs

I can listen for the main idea.

1 Do the Jungle Survival Quiz in pairs. Check your score. How long could you survive in the jungle?

2 3.7 Copy and complete the table. Use the adjectives in the box and the adverbs in blue in the quiz. Listen, check and repeat.

~~angry~~ easy fast good happy hard
hungry loud quick quiet slow

Adjective	Adverb
angry	*angrily*

3 Read the **Look!** box. What is the adverb form of these adjectives: *bad, heavy, nervous*?

Look! Adjectives and adverbs

Adjectives describe a noun: *The cat was **angry**.*
Adverbs describe a verb: *The cat looked at me **angrily**.*
To form adverbs, we often add *-ly* to the adjective: *quiet - quietly.*
Some words are both adjectives and adverbs: *fast, hard, late.*

4 Work in pairs. Choose an adverb from Exercise 1. Think of an action and an adverb and mime it. Can your partner guess what you are doing?

A: Are you reading a book quickly?
B: That's right!

5 3.8 Read the guide to a radio show, then listen. How many dangerous situations does Megan talk about? When and where did each one happen?

Radio 7
18:00 Amazing Adventures
Interview with the survival expert and TV presenter, Megan Turner.

6 3.8 Match 1–6 to a–f. Listen again and check.

1 Megan
2 The fast water
3 A cameraman
4 Megan and her team
5 An elephant
6 The driver of the jeep

a ran towards them.
b drove away fast.
c was swimming in the river.
d were filming elephants.
e rescued her.
f pulled her under.

JUNGLE SURVIVAL QUIZ

The jungle is a scary place. How long could you survive there? Try our quiz to find out!

1 You're walking through the jungle. There's a snake on the path in front of you. What do you do?
A Move the snake angrily with a stick and run away?
B Walk away slowly?

2 You hear a noise behind some trees. What do you do?
A Run fast towards the noise and get ready to fight. It could be food!
B Sit quietly until you know what's making the noise.

3 You see some colourful insects on a tree. What do you do?
A Eat them happily. You need the protein.
B Don't eat them. Colourful insects are often poisonous.

4 A jaguar is looking at you hungrily. What do you do?
A Turn and run through the jungle?
B Shout at it loudly to frighten it?

5 What survival skills have you got?
A I can easily complete all the levels in any video game!
B I can work hard, think quickly and plan well.

Mostly As: Oh dear! You probably couldn't survive 24 hours in the jungle!
Mostly Bs: You're the king/queen of the jungle! You could survive for months if you need to!

LS Language summary: Unit 3 SB p. 129

GRAMMAR Past simple and past continuous

I can use the past simple and the past continuous to talk about interrupted actions in the past.

Now watch the grammar animation.

1 Read the grammar box. Copy and complete the rules with *past simple* and *past continuous*.

I **was swimming** back to the camp **when** I **hit** my head on a rock.
While we **were filming**, an elephant **attacked** us.

I was swimming
We were filming

now

I hit my head
an elephant attacked us

Rules

We use different tenses to talk about a short completed action that interrupts a longer action in progress in the past.
We use the [1] ... for the longer action.
We use the [2] ... for the short action.
We often use *when* before the [3] ... .
We often use *while* before the [4] ... .

2 Copy and complete the sentences about some other moments in Megan's life.

While they (camp) in the jungle, they (see) a lot of snakes.
While they were camping in the jungle, they saw a lot of snakes.

1 She (lose) her phone while they (film).
2 When she (wake up) one morning, a big spider (crawl) on her arm.
3 She (walk) in the forest when she (hear) a jaguar.
4 She (speak) Portuguese while they (travel) in Brazil.
5 Luckily, she (not see) any piranhas while she (swim) in the river.

3 Imagine you are an explorer. Write about your most interesting or scariest moments. Use the ideas in the box and your own ideas.

While I was travelling in Australia, I ate insects.

explore stay swim travel	Africa Australia South America the mountains	break eat hear lose

Past time expressions

I can talk about when things happened in the past.

4 Read the grammar box. Copy and complete the rules with *ago*, *last*, *yesterday* and *before*.

We were in Africa **a few years ago**.
I was in South America **last month**.
We flew back **yesterday evening**.
We finished filming **the day before yesterday**.

Rules

We use [1] ... + *morning* / *afternoon* / *evening* to talk about the day before today.
We use *the day* [2] ... *yesterday* to mean two days ago.
We use [3] ... + *night* / *week* / *month* / *year* to mean the most recent night, week, month or year.
We use a length of time + [4] ... to say when in the past something happened.

5 Put the expressions in the correct order. Start with the most recent expression.

two minutes ago, ...

a month ago a week ago last night last year
six years ago the day before yesterday
~~two minutes ago~~ yesterday afternoon

6 Complete the sentences with one word.

1 I went to Liverpool ... week to see my cousins.
2 She moved to a new house six months ... .
3 We went to the cinema ... afternoon.
4 I had a Maths exam the day ... yesterday.
5 What did you have for dinner ... night?

7 Read the dialogue. Work in pairs and make a new dialogue with the ideas in the box. Ask an extra question with *Why*, *Where*, *What*, *Who*, etc.

A: When did you last go to the cinema?
B: About three weeks ago.
A: What film did you see?
B: I saw Dr Dolittle!

buy some new trainers clean your room
eat spaghetti go on holiday go to the cinema
read a book take a photo on your phone

FUN FACT

Insects are full of protein and a great survival food! But it's best to cook them first!

FAST FINISHER

Write three more questions for the *Jungle Survival Quiz* on page 32.

LS Language summary: Unit 3 SB p. 129

Guess what happened!

READING and LISTENING

I can understand a news story.

1 Match the newspaper headlines with the stories.

1 **Rescuers save teenager from sea**

2 **Big surprise for British couple!**

3 **HONEST TEENAGER DOES THE RIGHT THING**

4 **SORRY I'M LATE. I WAS SAVING A MAN'S LIFE.**

a

Sixteen-year-old Sanjay Patel missed his first lesson yesterday, but he had a good excuse: he was helping to save someone's life. Sanjay was walking to school when he saw a man on the ground. The man was having a heart attack, but luckily Sanjay, a doctor's son, knew what to do. He gave the man CPR for ten minutes until an ambulance arrived. The man later thanked Sanjay from his hospital bed.

b

Two tourists were lucky to be alive after a whale nearly fell onto their boat. Jim and Nicole Gray, from the UK, were on a whale-watching trip in Alaska. They were in Glacier Bay when the huge whale suddenly jumped out of the water in front of them. 'We wanted to see whales,' said Nicole, 'but we didn't expect to be so close!'

c

Fourteen-year-old Henry Wood was walking home when he found a wallet in the street – with £500 inside! He couldn't find the owner's phone number, so he took the wallet to his local police station. The police told us they contacted the owner, who 'was very pleased'. The owner gave Henry £50 to thank him.

d

A young surfer was safe at home last night after he lost his surfboard in the water and couldn't swim back. A member of the public, Daisy Morris, was walking along the beach when she heard the teenager. 'He was shouting for help,' she said. Daisy immediately phoned 999. The lifeboat team arrived ten minutes later, and took the surfer safely to the lifeboat station.

2 Read the stories again and answer the questions.

1. How did Sanjay know what to do?
2. Why were Jim and Nicole in Alaska?
3. Where was Henry when he found the money?
4. How did Daisy know that the surfer was having problems?
5. What number do you call in an emergency in the UK?

3 COMPARE CULTURES **What number do you call in an emergency in your country? What are the different types of emergency services?**

4 3.9 **Listen to the emergency 999 call. Who is the girl phoning about?**

5 3.9 **Listen again and complete the form.**

Emergency 999 Call

Service: 1 …
Address of emergency: 2 …
What happened? 3 …
Name: 4 …
Age: 5 …

SPEAKING Telling a story and reacting

I can tell a story and react to someone else's story.

1 3.10 **Listen and read. Which story from page 34 is it? What does the girl suggest at the end?**

Henry: Guess what happened yesterday!
Lina: What?
Henry: I was walking home from school when I found a wallet in the street.
Lina: No way! What did you do?
Henry: I opened it. You aren't going to believe this, but there was £500 inside.
Lina: You're kidding!
Henry: No, really. I looked in the wallet for a phone number, but I couldn't find one.
Lina: What happened next?
Henry: I took the wallet to the police station and they managed to contact the owner. He gave me £50 to say thank you.
Lina: Wow, that's amazing! So, shall we go for a pizza then? You're paying!

2 3.11 **Listen and repeat the Useful language.**

Useful language

Telling a story

Guess what happened yesterday/ last weekend/ on Wednesday!
I was ... when I ...
You aren't going to believe this, but ...
No, really.

Reacting

No way!
You're kidding!
What happened next?
Wow, that's amazing!

3 3.12 **Copy and complete the new dialogue with the phrases. There are two extra phrases. Listen and check.**

a You're kidding!
b What day was it?
c What?
d What happened next?
e Where did it happen?
f No way! What did you do?

Carly: Guess what happened on Saturday!
Rohan: 1 ...
Carly: Our cat ran up a tree and couldn't get down.
Rohan: 2 ...
Carly: We tried to rescue her, but we couldn't. She just sat there, miaowing loudly.
Rohan: 3 ...
Carly: Our neighbour helped us. He had a ladder and climbed up the tree. But while he was climbing up, our cat decided to jump down!
Rohan: 4 ...
Carly: No, really. I think she was scared of our neighbour!

4 **Work in pairs. Tell and react to an interesting story. Follow the steps in the Speaking plan.**

Speaking plan

Prepare

- Think of a time when something interesting or unbelievable happened to you, or choose one of the news stories from page 34 and imagine this happened to you.
- Decide on your roles and make notes for your dialogue.

Speak

- Practise your dialogue.
- Use phrases from the **Useful language** box.
- Act out your dialogue without notes.

Reflect

- How can you improve next time?
- Choose a different news story and swap roles.

Now play *Keep moving!*

FAST FINISHER

Think of an exciting news story you heard about recently. Write what you remember about it.

I heard that there's going to be a new restaurant opening in our town ...

LS Language summary: Unit 3 SB p. 129

REAL CULTURE!

Australia's dangerous animals

I can compare animals in my country with animals in Australia.

DANGER DOWN UNDER!

Australia is a beautiful country with rainforests, incredible beaches and cool cities. It's home to some amazing animals, for example, kangaroos, koalas and platypuses, but if you're planning a visit, here are some animals that you definitely don't want to meet!

Sharks

There are about 180 types of shark in the oceans around Australia. The most dangerous is the great white shark. They aren't the largest sharks, but they can grow up to seven metres long – that's almost as long as a bus![1] ... They eat fish, seals and small whales, but don't worry – sharks don't often attack humans.[2] ...

Snakes

Snakes are shy creatures and don't normally attack humans. However, there are lots of poisonous snakes in Australia so you need to be careful. The most poisonous is the inland taipan.[3] ... It lives in the Australian Outback and eats mostly rats.[4] ... Its poison is strong enough to kill a human within 45 minutes, but because it lives in rocky areas that are hard to get to, attacks on humans are very unusual.

Spiders

The Sydney funnel-web spider is the most poisonous spider in Australia. They sometimes attack people (there are about 30–40 bites each year), but people don't usually die from their bite.[5] ... The spiders live under rocks and logs where it's cool and wet, and they run out to catch lizards, beetles and other small animals.[6] ... They don't live indoors, but they sometimes walk into people's houses or fall into swimming pools, where they can survive for many hours. So, before you dive into the pool, always check the water!

1 Look at the pictures on page 36. What do the animals have in common?

2 3.13 Read and listen to the article. Copy and complete the table for each of the animals below:

- great white shark
- inland taipan
- Sydney funnel-web spider

Name of animal	
Where does it live?	
What does it eat?	
Does it often attack humans?	

3 Complete the article with sentences a–f.

a However, if you see a sign at the beach, don't go in the water!
b They then return to eat their meal.
c It also sometimes eats other small mammals and birds.
d It's green and brown in colour and can grow up to 2.4 metres long.
e These creatures have huge mouths with 300 very sharp teeth!
f However, it's important to get to a hospital quickly.

4 Word Power Copy and complete the table with animals from the text. Work in pairs. How many more animals can you add?

Mammals	*kangaroo,* 1 …
Insects	2 …
Reptiles	3 …
Fish	4 …
Other	5 …

5 3.14 Do the crocodile quiz. Listen and check your answers.

6 Are there any dangerous animals in your country? What are they? Where do they live? What do they eat?

Now watch the culture video.

FAST FINISHER
Write some quiz questions about an animal from your country.

CRIKEY! IT'S A CROC!

Australia is also home to the world's largest reptile, the saltwater crocodile. Are you brave enough to take our crocodile quiz?

1 Where do saltwater crocodiles live?
a In the sea
b In rivers and lakes
c In rivers and in the sea

2 How long can they grow?
a Up to four metres
b Up to seven metres
c Up to twenty metres

3 How many teeth do they have?
a 64–68 b 30–34 c 16–20

4 What do they eat?
a Mostly plants
b Mostly fish
c Fish, birds and mammals

5 How long do they live?
a Up to 30 years
b Up to 100 years
c Up to 200 years

6 When did crocodiles first appear on Earth?
a 2 million years ago
b 20 million years ago
c 200 million years ago

A rescue story

WRITING A narrative

I can write a short story.

1 **Read the story. When and where did the rescue happen? Who needed the helicopter and why?**

HELICOPTER RESCUE

Last weekend, I went camping with my family in Wales. The campsite was on top of some cliffs, with a lovely beach below. When we arrived, it was late, so we went straight to bed! During the night, it rained heavily.

The next morning, it was a beautiful sunny day, and we decided to go to the beach. The path down the cliffs was muddy from all the rain. We were walking down the path slowly and carefully when suddenly a man in front of us fell and hurt his leg. He couldn't move, so we called 999 and asked for an ambulance.

While we were waiting, we heard the sound of a helicopter. The ambulance couldn't reach us, so they sent a helicopter instead! The rescue team pulled the man up into the helicopter and took him to hospital. They said his leg was broken, but he was OK. We spent the rest of the day at the beach – what a weekend!

2 Look at the **Useful language**. How do you say these expressions in your language?

Useful language

Writing a story

Last weekend/month/summer, ...
When we arrived, it was (late).
We were (walking down the path) (slowly) when suddenly ...
While we were (waiting), ...
What a weekend/day/holiday!

3 **Read the Look! box. Complete the rules with *when, while* and *during*. Look at page 33 to help you.**

Look! ***when, while, during***

We use *when, while* and *during* to talk about something that happened in the past.

We were walking down the path ***when*** *suddenly a man in front of us fell.*

While *we were waiting, we heard the sound of a helicopter.*

During *the night, it rained heavily.*

Rules

We usually use [1]... + longer actions.
We use [2]... + a noun.
We usually use [3]... + short actions.

4 **Choose the correct word in each sentence.**

1 She was running down the street *when / while* she dropped her phone.
2 They got lost *while / during* they were walking in the mountains.
3 It started snowing *while / during* the journey.
4 He was cycling into town *when / while* he fell off.
5 *While / During* we were swimming, we saw a dolphin.

5 **Write a rescue story about one of the situations below or your own idea. Follow the steps in the Writing plan.**

- You were walking in the mountains with a friend when you got lost.
- You were on a skiing holiday when your friend had an accident.
- You were kayaking in the sea when your boat hit some rocks.
- You were camping in the forest when a snake bit your friend.

Writing plan

Prepare

› Make notes for your story: When did it happen? Where were you? What was the weather like? What happened in the end? Was there a rescue?

Write

› Organize your ideas into paragraphs:
  • Introduction • The accident/problem
  • The rescue/ending
› Use the expressions from the **Useful language** box.

Check

› Check your grammar: past simple and continuous.
› Check *when, while* and *during*.
› Check your spelling.

W Writing summary WB p. 86
R Review: Units 1-3 SB pp. 100–101
P Project: Units 1-3 SB pp. 106–107
L Literature: Units 1-3 SB pp. 112–113
E Exams: Unit 3 SB p. 120
LS Language summary: Unit 3 SB p. 129

Consumer society

4

Vocabulary: Containers; Money verbs | **Grammar:** Quantifiers; Comparatives and superlatives; *(not) as ... as* | **Speaking:** Comparing products | **Writing:** A survey

VOCABULARY Containers

I can talk about food and drink containers.

1 4.1 **Match the words in the boxes with the pictures above. Listen, check and repeat.**

1 a glass of milk

bag	bottle	bowl	box	can	carton
cup	~~glass~~	jar	packet	tin	tube

biscuits cereal coffee crisps fizzy drink
jam ~~milk~~ orange juice soup tomatoes
tomato sauce toothpaste

2 Think of containers for the products in the box.

a bowl of rice / a packet of rice

beans olives peanuts pineapple juice
~~rice~~ shampoo sweets tea

3 In pairs, think of more products for the containers in Exercise 1. Who can make the longest list?

4 Work in pairs. Ask and answer the questions.

QUESTIONNAIRE

1. How many glasses of water do you drink in a day?
2. How many bags of crisps do you eat in a week?
3. How many cans of fizzy drink do you drink in a year?
4. Do you sometimes carry a bottle of water? Where?
5. What's your favourite cinema treat: a box of popcorn, a bag of sweets or a packet of peanuts?

Now watch the vlog.

FAST FINISHER

Imagine you're going camping for the weekend with some friends. Make a list of food, drink and other things to take with you.

Food: a packet of pasta, ...

LS **Language summary: Unit 4** **SB** p. 130

Love food, hate waste!

READING

I can use pictures to help me understand a text.

1 Look at the pictures and the title of Ella's diary. What do you think *waste* means?

MY FOOD WASTE DIARY

Around the world, we throw away one third of all the food that we produce – about 1.3 billion tonnes a year. Supermarkets waste a lot of food, but we also waste a lot of food at home. We asked fourteen-year-old Ella to keep a diary.

MONDAY

Breakfast

I usually have a bowl of cereal for breakfast, but today the milk tasted horrible. I threw my cereal away and had some toast instead.

Lunch

I had a music lesson, so I didn't have much time for lunch. There's usually quite a lot of choice in the school canteen, but when I got there, there wasn't much food left. I bought a slice of pizza and some yoghurt. The pizza was cold and I only ate half of it.

Snack

I was hungry when I got home, so I opened a packet of biscuits! How many did I have? Not many – two or three. OK, four!

Dinner

Dad cooked chicken with potatoes and vegetables. I ate some peas, but I didn't have any carrots – I'm not keen on them. For pudding, it was cherry pie. I took a big piece, but after too many biscuits earlier, I couldn't finish it. I threw the rest in the bin.

Final thoughts

I feel bad about the amount of food I wasted in just one day. It's bad for the environment and there are a lot of people who don't even have enough to eat. I want to be more careful … starting tomorrow!

2 4.2 **Read and listen to the diary and answer the questions.**

1 How much food do people waste every year?
2 Make a list of all the food that Ella wasted in one day.
3 Why does Ella think it's bad to waste food?

3 **Read the diary again. Which food didn't Ella eat because …**

1 it tasted bad?
2 it was cold?
3 she doesn't like them?
4 she was full?

4 **Word Power** **Work in pairs. Which is the odd word out in each group? Explain your answers. There may be more than one possible answer.**

1	milk	yoghurt	cheese	lemon
2	chicken	jam	burger	steak
3	carrot	bean	cherry	pea
4	apple	banana	orange	biscuit

5 **Work in pairs. Do you or your family sometimes waste food? How? What could people do to waste less food?**

6 **FIND OUT** **There are some eggs in the fridge, but you don't know if they're good or bad to eat. How can you use a bowl of water to find out?**

GRAMMAR Quantifiers: *some, any, (how) much, (how) many, a lot of*

I can talk about quantities.

Now watch the grammar animation.

1 **Read the grammar box. Copy and complete the rules with the words in the box.**

affirmative (x2) countable negative (x2)
questions uncountable

Countable nouns	Uncountable nouns
Affirmative	
I ate **some** peas. There are **a lot of** people.	I had **some** toast. There's **a lot of** choice.
Negative	
I didn't have **any** carrots. I didn't eat **many** / **a lot of** biscuits.	There isn't **any** milk. I didn't have **much** / **a lot of** time.
Questions	
Are there **any** apples? Has he got **many** / **a lot of** friends? **How many** biscuits did I have?	Do you do **any** exercise? Was there **much** / **a lot of** food? **How much** money have you got?

Rules

We use *some* and *a lot of* in [1] ... sentences.

We use *any* in [2] ... sentences and [3] ... .

With [4] ... nouns, we use *much* in negative sentences and questions.

With [5] ... nouns, we use *many* in negative sentences and questions.

We can use *a lot of* in [6] ... and [7] ... sentences, and in questions.

2 **Choose the correct answer.**

1 Emilia didn't give her brother *any / many / some* help.
2 There are *a lot of / any / much* students at my school.
3 My dad doesn't have *many / much / some* free time.
4 How *many / much / a lot of* bottles of water do we need?
5 They haven't got *many / much / some* video games in this shop.
6 We do *a lot of / any / much* sport at my school.
7 I dropped *any / much / some* food on the floor.
8 Do you do *many / much / some* exercise?

3 **PRONUNCIATION** **The letter *a***

4.3 **Listen to how we pronounce the letter *a* in these words. Listen again and repeat.**

/æ/	/eɪ/	/ɑː/	/e/
packet	waste	half	any

4 4.4 **Put these words in the correct column in Exercise 3. Listen, check and repeat.**

anything apple ate carton
dad glass many taste

5 4.5 **Complete the interview with the words in the box. Listen and check.**

a lot of any How many How much
much some (x2)

THE WASTE FOOD RESTAURANT

Alex Smith is a young chef with an unusual restaurant – it only uses waste food. We asked him about it.

What's the idea of the restaurant?
Supermarkets throw away [1] ... food every day, and most of it is still good to eat. Supermarkets give us the food, and we cook [2] ... delicious meals with it.

What sort of meals do you cook?
The menu is different every day. A lot of our customers are vegetarians or vegans, so there's always an option that doesn't have [3] ... meat.

[4] ... does it cost to eat there?
People pay what they want. If a customer doesn't have [5] ... money, they only pay a small amount.

[6] ... people eat at the restaurant?
About 300 people a week. At the moment, we're very small, but we've got [7] ... big plans!

6 **GET CREATIVE** **Work in groups. Create some posters for your school about the problem of waste food. What can we do to waste less?**

FAST FINISHER

What's in your fridge at home? Write four sentences using quantifiers.

I think there's some cheese. There aren't any pizzas.

LS Language summary: Unit 4 SB p. 130

Are you good with money?

VOCABULARY and LISTENING Money verbs

I can listen for different ideas in a radio programme.

1

2

3

4

5

6

7

8

9

10

1 4.6 **Match the sentences with the pictures. Listen and check.**

a She's buying an ice cream.
b He's selling balloons.
c She's earning money by cleaning cars.
d They're shopping online for some clothes.
e The jeans cost £30.
f She's paying by card.
g He's spending his pocket money on sweets.
h He's saving his money.
i She's lending some money to her friend.
j He's borrowing some money from his dad.

2 Work in pairs. Ask and answer the questions.

1 If you have some money, do you usually spend it or save it?
2 Do you do jobs to earn extra money?
3 Do you sometimes borrow things from your friends? What sort of things?
4 Do you pay for things by card?

3 4.7 **Listen to an interview with two teenagers, Lydia and Dylan. How much pocket money do they each get? What do they do with their money?**

4 4.7 **Read the ideas in *How to look after your money*. Listen again. Which ideas do Lydia and Dylan mention?**

TOP TIPS
How to look after your money

- Pay in cash rather than by card. ☐
- Always look for the best prices. ☐
- Go shopping with your parents. ☐
- Shop online. ☐
- Save your money for things that you really want. ☐
- Don't buy things that you don't need. ☐

5 Work in pairs. Are you good with money? Which of the ideas in Exercise 4 do you do? Can you think of any other tips?

LS Language summary: Unit 4 SB p. 130

GRAMMAR Comparatives and superlatives; *(not) as ... as*

I can compare things.

Now watch the grammar animation.

1 Read the grammar box. Copy and complete the grammar box with words from the interview on page 42.

Adjective	Comparative	Superlative
Short adjectives		
cheap	[1] ...	**the cheapest**
big	bigger	**the biggest**
easy	[2] ...	**the easiest**
Long adjectives		
relaxing	[3] ...	**the most** relaxing
Irregular adjectives		
good	[4] ...	**the best**
bad	**worse**	**the worst**
far	**further**	**the furthest**

2 Choose the correct answer.

1 I bought *cheapest* / *the cheapest* jeans in the shop.
2 It's *easier* / *easiest* to spend money than to save it!
3 Hong Kong is the *more* / *most* expensive city in the world.
4 Actors earn a lot of money, but footballers' salaries are often *higher* / *highest*.
5 Friends are more important *than* / *that* money.
6 This is *worse* / *the worst* restaurant in the world!

3 Read the grammar box. Choose the correct answers in the rules.

(not) as ... as

I'm **as tall as** my dad.
The bus was **as quick as** the train.
My phone is**n't as fast as** a new phone.
The film was**n't as good as** the book.

Rules

We use *as* + adjective + *as* to compare two things that are [1] *the same* / *different*.

We use *not as* + adjective + *as* to compare two things that are [2] *the same* / *different*.

4 Complete each second sentence so that it means the same as the first sentence.

A Ferrari is faster than a cheetah.
A cheetah isn't as fast as a Ferrari.

1 The waiter was friendlier than the manager.
The manager ...
2 My mum's phone was more expensive than my phone.
My phone ...
3 In my opinion, football is more exciting than golf.
In my opinion, golf ...
4 My parents aren't as funny as your parents.
Your parents ...
5 The bus station isn't as far as the train station.
The train station ...

5 Complete the article. Use the correct form of the adjective in brackets.

Would you like to go shopping in a place that is [1] ... (big) as 50 football pitches? The Dubai Mall is one of [2] ... (large) shopping malls in the world. It's next to [3] ... (tall) building in the world, the Burj Khalifa. The mall contains an aquarium, an ice rink and 120 restaurants. There are more than 1,200 shops, including one of [4] ... (good) sweet shops in the world. The shops are [5] ... (expensive) than a lot of other places, but that doesn't stop the 80 million people that visit it every year. Wow – 80 million visitors a year – that's crazy! Even New York City isn't [6] ... (popular) as the Dubai Mall!

6 THINK CRITICALLY What are the advantages and disadvantages of shopping malls compared to small shops and markets? How do you prefer to shop and why?

7 Work in small groups. Use the adjectives to compare your opinions about the topics.

films food music shops sports teams TV programmes video games

boring enjoyable exciting good interesting scary strange tasty

A: I think heavy metal is better than rap music.
B: I don't agree. Heavy metal isn't as exciting as rap.
C: Maybe, but dance music is the best!

FUN FACT

The inventor of the shopping mall, Victor Gruen, hated his invention. 'They destroyed our cities,' he said later in his life.

FAST FINISHER

Write sentences comparing famous people.

Taylor Swift is taller than Selena Gomez. She's a better singer, too.

LS Language summary: Unit 4 SB p. 130

KEEP TALKING!

Too much choice?

READING and LISTENING

I can understand product reviews.

GEORGE'S GADGET GUIDE

Welcome to my gadget guide! This week I'm reviewing wireless speakers, sports action cameras and hoverboards.

Wireless Speakers

XR MegaPlay

Great price

The MegaPlay speaker is small and waterproof, so you can play your favourite tunes anywhere, even in the shower! The thing I like most about it is the price.

Size: 7 cm x 7 cm x 5 cm
Volume: 🔈🔈🔈🔈
Price: £19.99
Colours: orange, blue, green

JMC SoundBox

Best sound

The SoundBox has a powerful sound, so it's great for parties! It's even got coloured lights! The only problem is it's quite heavy, so it isn't easy to carry.

Size: 30 cm x 9 cm x 12 cm
Volume: 🔈🔈🔈🔈🔈
Price: £79.99
Colours: black, blue, grey

Sports Action Cameras

Epic V2

Easy to use

The Epic V2 is voice-controlled, so it's very easy to use. You can't take it in water, but it's perfect for using on your bike or scooter!

Easy to use: 😊😊😊😊😊
Weight: 95 g
Price: £35.99
Colours: blue, pink, grey

Active-Pro CS

Water-proof

The Active-Pro CS is completely waterproof. You can make great videos, and with the free app, you can upload them online immediately.

Easy to use: 😊😊😊😊
Weight: 500 g
Price: £74.99
Colours: orange, yellow, white

Hoverboards

JetBoard V8

Fastest board

This is one of the fastest hoverboards you can buy, so it's only for experienced riders. It's quite noisy, so don't ride it up and down your street.

Speed: Up to 22 km per hour
Safety: 👍
Price: £219.00
Colours: yellow, orange, green

MaxFly Plus

Safest ride

The MaxFly Plus is fast, but not too fast, so it feels very safe. It's got lights so that people can see you at night, and it's very quiet. I love this board!

Speed: Up to 12 km per hour
Safety: 👍👍👍
Price: £99.99
Colours: purple, orange, blue

1 **Look at the web page. What sort of text is it? Choose from the answers below. Then read quickly and check.**

a an online shop
b a blog with reviews of products
c an instruction book

2 **Read the web page again and answer the questions.**

1 What's the best thing about the MegaPlay speaker, in George's opinion?
2 What doesn't George like about the SoundBox speaker?
3 Which is the best camera if you want to share videos with friends quickly?
4 Why is the Epic V2 camera easy to use?
5 Which hoverboard is the best for beginners?
6 Give three reasons why George loves the MaxFly Plus.

3 **Look at the words in blue in the text. Which word tells us if something is …**

expensive or cheap? *price*

1 big or small?
2 fast or slow?
3 heavy or light?
4 loud or quiet?

4 🔊 4.8 **Listen to *Polly's Podcast*. What is Polly reviewing today? Which of the two products does she like the best?**

5 🔊 4.8 **Listen again. Copy and complete the table.**

	MaxPack	NiceDay
Size	very big	4 … and …
Weight	1 …	light
Colours	blue, 2 … and black	5 …, orange and green
Price	3 £ …	6 £ …

SPEAKING Comparing products

I can compare the advantages and disadvantages of two different products.

1 4.9 **Listen, read and answer the questions.**

1 Which wireless speaker on page 44 does Lottie decide to buy?
2 What are her reasons for choosing the speaker?
3 Where did she get the money from?

Isaac: Hi, Lottie. What are you up to?
Lottie: I'm looking for a new wireless speaker – I got some money for my birthday.
Isaac: Cool! Which one are you thinking of getting?
Lottie: I'm not sure. What do you think of this one?
Isaac: The JMC Soundbox? It looks nice, but it's quite expensive. The XR MegaPlay is much cheaper.
Lottie: You're right, but it isn't as powerful as the Soundbox.
Isaac: Yes, but the MegaPlay is smaller, so it's easier to carry.
Lottie: That's true. OK, which colour do you prefer?
Isaac: I prefer blue. I think it's a cool colour for a speaker.
Lottie: I agree. I like blue, too. Right, I'm going to get the MegaPlay in blue.

2 4.10 **Listen and repeat the Useful language.**

Useful language

Asking opinions
What do you think of this one/these ones?
Which colour do you prefer?

Comparing
It looks/They look ..., but it's/they're ...
The ... is/are much ...
It isn't/They aren't as ... as the ...

Agreeing
You're right. / That's true. / I agree.

3 4.11 **Copy and complete the dialogue in a sports shop with the words in the box. Listen and check.**

agree cheaper comfortable heavier prefer true

Zoe: I'm looking for some new trainers. What do you think of these ones?
Theo: The SuperZooms? They look good, but they're quite expensive. These QuickRuns are [1] ... .
Zoe: Yes, but they're much [2] ... and they aren't as cool.
Theo: That's [3] ... .
Zoe: The SuperZooms are more [4] ... . Which colour do you [5] ...?
Theo: I like orange.
Zoe: I [6] ... . I'm going to get them in orange.

4 **Work in pairs. Compare two different products and choose the one you like most. Follow the steps in the Speaking plan.**

Speaking plan

Prepare
- Decide on your roles.
- Use *George's Gadget Guide* on page 44, or choose your own products.
- Make notes for your dialogue.

Speak
- Practise your dialogue.
- Use phrases from the **Useful language** box.
- Act out your dialogue without notes.

Reflect
- How can you improve next time?
- Swap roles and choose a new gadget.

Now play *Keep moving!*

FAST FINISHER

What's your favourite gadget at home? Write sentences about what you use it for, and how it compares with other gadgets.

My favourite gadget is my tablet. It's much lighter than my mum's laptop and I use it for playing games and listening to music ...

LS Language summary: Unit 4 SB p. 130

EXPLORE CULTURE!

Second-hand shopping in the UK

I can compare second-hand shopping in the UK with shopping in my country.

Luna's Blog

Home About Latest posts

Second-hand shopping is very popular in the UK. Here are the best places to look for a bargain!

Charity shops

I love charity shops. You can find them in every British town and city. People give old clothes, books, toys and other items to the shop, and the shop then sells them for charity. Everything is really cheap and usually good quality, and when you spend money there, you know that you're helping other people. The only problem is that you sometimes don't find anything you want, but if you're like me, that doesn't often happen!

Car boot sales

A car boot sale is where people come together and sell the things they don't want any more, usually from the boot of their car. You can find everything from books to bikes, and comics to computers. Car boot sales are often much cheaper than charity shops and the sellers will sometimes accept a lower price if you ask nicely! There are hundreds of sellers, so you can often find what you're looking for, but you need to get up early or you'll miss the best things.

Online platforms and apps

Online platforms and apps are a popular way to buy second-hand clothes. Users upload pictures of clothes that they own, and sell them directly to other users. It's better for the planet: why throw something away when you can still wear it? The apps are easy to use, and you can shop from your sofa! The clothes are usually more expensive than charity shops and car boot sales, but you need to be careful. There are sometimes dishonest sellers who take your money and then don't send you the clothes.

1 4.12 **Read and listen to Luna's blog about the best places to buy second-hand things. Which of the places is usually the cheapest? Which is usually the most expensive?**

2 **Read the blog again. Copy and complete the table, according to Luna.**

	Advantages	Disadvantages
Charity shops		
Car boot sales		
Online platforms and apps		

3 **Word Power** **Find words 1–7 in the text. Match them with definitions a–g.**

1 bargain
2 toy
3 good quality
4 boot
5 seller
6 upload
7 dishonest

a something that a child plays with
b to put something on the internet
c a person who sells something
d made well with good materials
e something that is much cheaper than usual
f not honest
g the space at the back of a car where you put suitcases, bags, etc.

4 **COMPARE CULTURES** **Discuss the questions as a class.**

1 Are there charity shops or car boot sales in your country?
2 What do people do with things they don't want any more?
3 Do you sometimes buy second-hand things? Why/Why not?

5 4.13 **Listen to the dialogue. Luna went shopping with some friends last Saturday. Where did they go? What did they do afterwards?**

6 4.13 **Listen again and match the people with the kinds of thing they bought. There are two extra things.**

1 Luna
2 David
3 Freddie
4 Georgia
5 Milly

Now watch the culture video.

FAST FINISHER

Have you got a lot of things that you don't want any more? Imagine you're going to have a car boot sale. Make a list of all the things you want to sell.

My old football kit, some toys I had when I was a baby, …

Your money and you

WRITING A survey

I can write about the results of a survey.

1 **Read the results of a survey. Which sentences are true for you?**

A SURVEY: YOUR MONEY AND YOU

Last week, we did a class survey about teenagers and their money. We interviewed fifteen people and asked three questions. Here are the results.

HOW MUCH POCKET MONEY DO YOU GET A WEEK?

A few students don't get any pocket money, but most students get about £8 a week. Almost everybody gets their pocket money in cash, but a couple of students have bank accounts and their parents pay the money into their account.

DO YOU GET MONEY FROM ANYWHERE ELSE?

Half of the students get money from parents or relatives on their birthday or other special occasions. Some students earn extra money by doing jobs around the house. Nobody has a weekend job.

WHAT DO YOU SPEND YOUR MONEY ON?

The most popular answers were clothes, snacks, games and make-up. A few students try and save some money to buy more expensive things, such as phones or games consoles.

2 **Look at the Useful language. How do you say these expressions in your language?**

Useful language

Survey results

Last week, we did a class survey about ...
We interviewed ...
Here are the results.
The most popular answers were ...

3 **Read the Look! box. Find examples in the text. Which of the expressions are followed by a plural verb? Which are followed by a singular verb?**

Look! Expressions of quantity

Everybody
Most students
Half of the students
Some students
A few students
A couple of students
Nobody

4 **Look at the graph showing how ten students use their mobile phones. Copy and complete the sentences with the correct expressions of quantity.**

HOW DO YOU USE YOUR MOBILE PHONE?

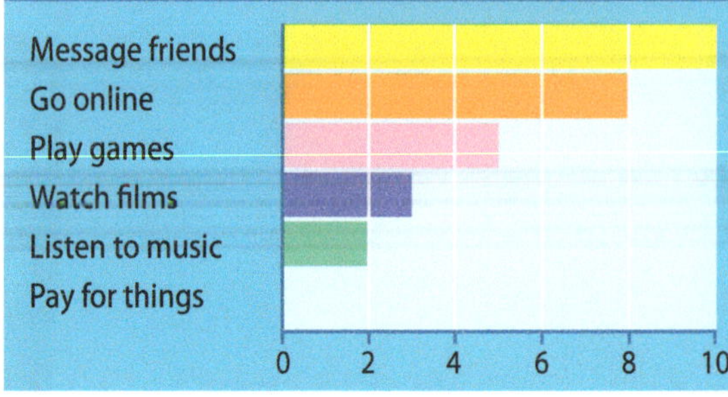

Half of the students play games on their phones.

1 ... students watch films.
2 ... students use their phone to go online.
3 ... uses it to pay for things.
4 ... students listen to music.
5 ... uses it to message their friends.

5 **Work in small groups. Write a survey report. Follow the steps in the Writing plan.**

A survey: Exercise and you

1 How much exercise do you do a week?

0–1 hour 1–2 hours 2–3 hours 3 hours or more

2 What is your favourite form of exercise?

Ball sports Gymnastics or dance Swimming Athletics Cycling

3 Where do you usually do exercise?

At school At a club At the park At a sports centre

Writing plan

Prepare

› Imagine that you interviewed ten people in your class about exercise. Look at the three questions above, and the possible answers.
› Invent the results. Out of the ten people you interviewed, how many chose each answer?

Write

› Organize your ideas into paragraphs:
  - In the introduction, say what the survey was about and how many people you interviewed.
  - Use a different paragraph for each question, and use expressions of quantity to give the results.
› Use expressions from the **Useful language** box.

Check

› Check your grammar: quantifiers, comparatives and superlatives.
› Check expressions of quantity and your spelling.

W Writing summary WB p. 87 E Exams: Unit 4 SB p. 121 L Language summary: Unit 4 SB p. 130

I'm only human

5

Vocabulary: The human body; Health problems **Grammar:** *will* and *won't*, *may*; First conditional; *should/shouldn't* **Speaking:** Giving advice **Writing:** A *How to ...* guide

VOCABULARY The human body

I can talk about the human body.

1 5.1 **Match the words in the box with the picture. Listen, check and repeat.**

ankle bone brain elbow face
finger heart knee neck shoulder
skin stomach throat thumb toe

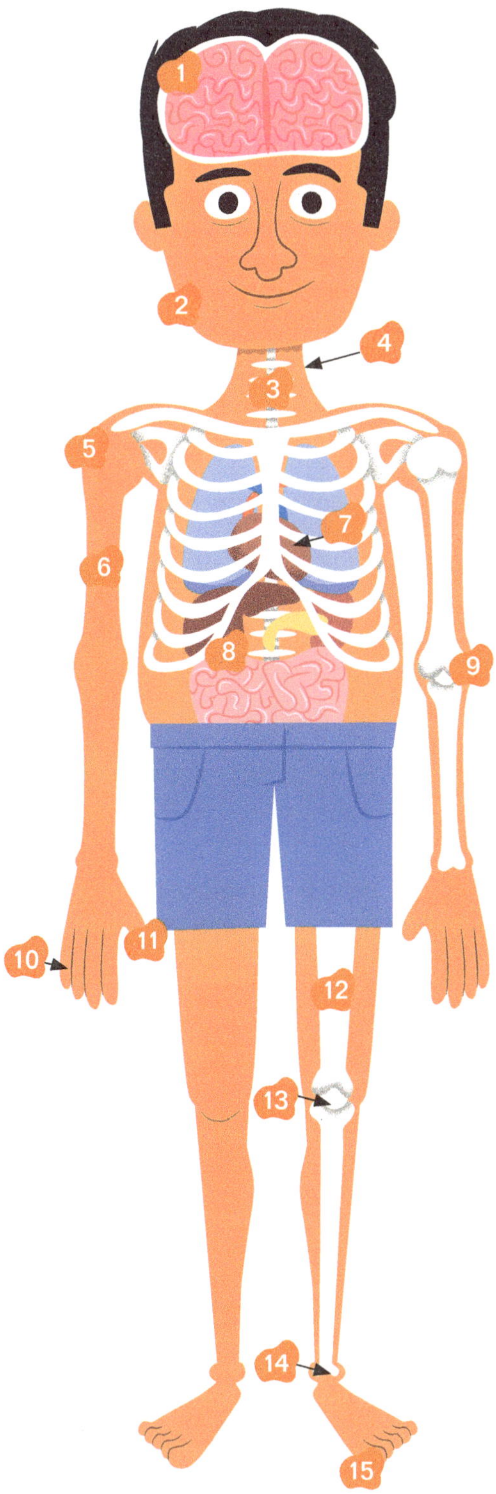

2 **Copy the table. Add the words from Exercise 1, and more parts of the body that you know. Which words can go in all three columns?**

Lower body	Upper body	Head
ankle	*finger*	*brain*

3 5.2 **Complete the facts in *The human body in numbers*. Use the numbers in the box. Listen and check.**

5 to 8 73 206 115,000 50 million

THE HUMAN BODY in numbers

There are [1] … bones in the human body.

Your heart beats about [2] … times a day.

The human brain is [3] … % water.

You lose [4] … skin cells every day.

When you eat, it takes about [5] … seconds for food to get from your throat to your stomach.

4 **Work in pairs. Read the sentences and identify the parts of the body. Write more sentences for your partner to guess.**

1 You have two of these, one on each hand.
2 These are at the top of your arms.
3 You wear a scarf around this when it's cold.
4 You use these to see.

Now watch the vlog.

FAST FINISHER

Invent a strange-looking alien. Draw it and write sentences.

My alien has got a large body with two very long necks and two heads. It's got …

LS Language summary: Unit 5 SB p. 131

Humans of the future

READING

I can work out the meaning of new words.

The face of the future?

Humans are evolving all the time. Today, we are about 10 cm taller than we were 150 years ago, and we are living longer and longer lives. So, what will humans be like in the future? Will robots make us lazier and fatter? Will we develop superpowers, such as X-ray vision or brain-to-brain communication? No one knows for sure, but here are some predictions.

A lot of scientists believe that in the future, we will live on other planets. This will create big changes in our bodies. For example, Mars has less gravity than Earth, so humans on Mars will probably be taller. Mars also receives less sunlight, so our eyes may grow bigger so that we can see better, and our brains and heads may become larger, too. It won't be easy to grow food on Mars, so a lot of our meals may come in pills. We may not need as many teeth, and our mouths may become smaller.

Other people predict that in the future, humans will evolve digitally. Scientists will use robotics and artificial intelligence to make superhumans or cyborgs. We will have mechanical arms and legs so that we can move and run faster, and we will connect our brains to computers so that we can control things with our thoughts. Some scientists even predict that we won't grow old or die because doctors will simply repair broken body parts. The big question then is: will we still be humans?

1 **Work in pairs. Read the predictions about humans in the future. Which do you think will happen?**

A We will all speak the same language.
B Humans will find new worlds to live on.
C Parents will choose what their babies look like.
D We will live forever.
E Our bodies will be part-human, part-machine.

2 **5.3 Read and listen to the article. Which of the predictions are mentioned in the text? What other predictions are in the text?**

3 **Read the article again. Find these words and work out the meaning. How do you say them in your language?**

1 develop
2 gravity
3 pills
4 predict
5 thoughts
6 repair

4 **Word Power We can sometimes add *-ion* to a verb to make a noun. Copy and complete the table.**

verb	noun
predict	*prediction*
create	creation
invent	1 …
2 …	action
pollute	3 …
4 …	discussion
communicate	5 …

5 **THINK CRITICALLY Are robots replacing humans? What are the advantages and disadvantages of having robots in our lives?**

6 **FIND OUT How far is it from Earth to Mars, when the two planets are closest to each other?**

GRAMMAR *will* and *won't*; *may*

I can make predictions about the future.

Now watch the grammar animation.

1 **Read the grammar box. Copy and complete the rule.**

Affirmative

I/You/He/She/It/We/They**'ll** be taller.

Negative

I/You/He/It/She/We/They **won't** grow old or die.

Questions	Short answers
Will we still be humans?	Yes, we **will**. / No, we **won't**.

Rules

We use *will* and *won't* to make predictions about the future. The contracted form of *will* is [1] … .

2 **Think about the world 50 years from now. Make your own predictions with *will* or *won't*.**

cars / need a driver
Cars won't need a driver.

1 robots / replace teachers
2 we / build homes under the sea
3 humans / live to be 200 years old
4 schools / exist
5 aliens / visit our planet
6 we / have holidays in space

3 **Read the Look! box. What is the difference between sentences a and b?**

a James will be at the party tonight.
b James may be at the party tonight.

Look! ***may* and *may not***

We use *may* (*not*) when we are not certain about a prediction.
*Our eyes **may** grow bigger.*
*We **may not** need as many teeth.*

4 **Choose the correct answer.**

1 Scientists *may* / *will* discover life on other planets – who knows?
2 I'm sure my mum *may* / *will* love these flowers.
3 Sam isn't very well. I'm not sure, but he *may not* / *won't* be in school tomorrow.
4 I *'ll* / *may* always love you! You know that, don't you?
5 I *may* / *will* play basketball later – it depends how much homework I've got.
6 Jack *will* / *may* be coming to visit this weekend. He's booked his train ticket!

5 5.4 **Put the words in the correct order to make questions. Listen and check.**

What will life be like in the 22nd century?

1 in our homes / have / will / What new technology / we / ?
2 travel / How / people / will / ?
3 people / will / wear / What type of clothes / ?
4 be / different / our food / How / will / ?
5 What / be / like / schools / will / ?
6 in our free time / do / we / What / will / ?

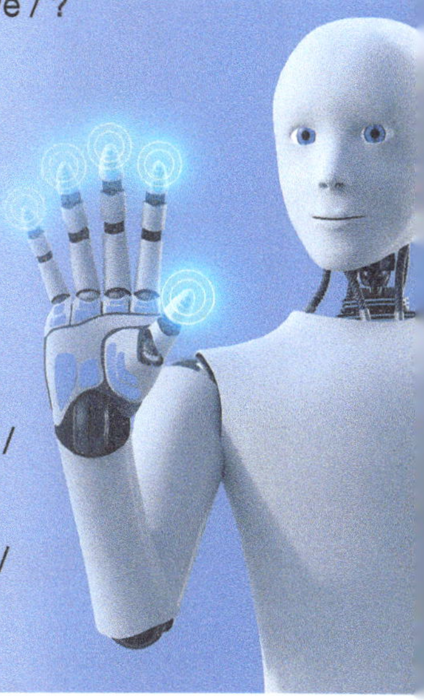

6 **Work in pairs. Ask and answer the questions in Exercise 5.**

A: What new technology will we have in our homes?
B: I think we'll have robots to do all the jobs around the home.
A: I agree. And we may have fridges that can order the shopping.

FUN FACT

Whales live in the sea, but 50 million years ago, their ancestors had legs and walked on land.

FAST FINISHER

Write more questions about the future like the ones in Exercise 5. Then write answers.

LS Language summary: Unit 5 SB p. 131

If you don't rest, you won't get better

VOCABULARY and LISTENING Health problems

I can identify the relationship between speakers in different situations.

1 5.5 **Match the problems in the box with the people. Listen, check and repeat.**

I've got a broken leg. I've got a cold. I've got a cough. I've got a headache. I've got a sore throat. I've got a stomach ache. I've got sunburn. I've got a temperature. I've got toothache. My back hurts.

2 Copy and complete the sentences.

1 Please stop shouting! I've got a ... .
2 She's got a ... of 38°C. She needs to stay in bed.
3 I've got really bad ... . I need to see a dentist.
4 I've got a ... . It hurts when I speak.
5 Don't stay on the beach for too long. You'll get ... .
6 I've got a ... . I think I ate too much at lunch.

3 Work in pairs. When did you, or a member of your family, last have any of the problems in Exercise 1?

A: I had a sore throat last week.

B: Really? My dad broke his leg two years ago.

4 5.6 **Listen to three dialogues. Where are the people in each dialogue? What is their relationship?**

5 5.6 **Listen again and answer the questions.**

1 What is Emma's problem?
2 Why doesn't she want to stay at home and rest?
3 On what part of his body has Tom got sunburn?
4 What is his mum's advice?
5 Why is Ali's back hurting?
6 What is the teacher's advice?

LS Language summary: Unit 5 SB p. 131

GRAMMAR First conditional

I can talk about situations and their results.

Now watch the grammar animation.

1 **Read the grammar box. Look at sentences a and b. Which parts are the situation, and which parts are the result?**

Situation	Result
If you **don't rest**,	you **won't get** better.
Result	**Situation**
It'**ll be** better for your team	if you **don't play**.

Rules

We use the first conditional to talk about situations and their results.

To describe the situation, we use *if* + present simple.

To describe the result, we use *will* or *won't* + infinitive.

We use a comma when the situation clause is at the start of the sentence.

a If you stay in the sun for too long, you'll get sunburn.

b Your bag won't be as heavy if you only carry the books you need.

2 **Copy and complete the sentences with the correct form of the verb in brackets.**

1 If she ... (eat) too many sweets, she'll get toothache.
2 Be careful! You ... (hurt) yourself if you fall off your skateboard.
3 If he doesn't take his medicine, he ... (not feel) better.
4 Other people will catch your cold if you ... (not stay) at home.
5 If we don't drink enough water, we ... (get) a headache.
6 If she doesn't get better soon, she ... (miss) the final.

3 **Complete the sentences in your notebook with your own ideas.**

1 If it's sunny at the weekend, ...
2 I'll be really happy if ...
3 If I'm hungry when I get home, ...
4 My parents will be really angry if ...
5 If I pass all my exams this year, ...
6 If I lose my phone on the way home, ...

4 **Work in pairs. Read one of your endings for the sentences in Exercise 3. Can your partner guess the sentence?**

should and *shouldn't*

I can use *should* and *shouldn't* to give advice.

5 **Read the grammar box. What form of the verb do we use after *should* and *shouldn't*?**

Affirmative	
I/You/He/She/We/They **should** stay at home and rest.	
Negative	
I/You/He/She/We/They **shouldn't** stay in the sun so long.	
Questions	**Short answers**
Should I put some cream on them?	Yes, you **should**. / No, you **shouldn't**.

6 **Complete the health advice with *should* or *shouldn't*.**

Top tips for a healthy heart

You [1] ... exercise every day.

You [2] ... smoke.

You [3] ... eat too much salt or fatty food.

You [4] ... eat plenty of fruit and vegetables.

You [5] ... look after your weight.

You [6] ... stay up late every night.

7 **PRONUNCIATION** /ʊ/ and /uː/

5.7 **Listen and repeat.**

/ʊ/	cook good put should
/uː/	do food true you

8 5.8 **In your notebook, add the words in the box to the table. Listen, check and repeat.**

blue book could foot
shoe soon tooth would

9 **Work in pairs. Take it in turns to ask for and give advice in these situations:**

- You've got a headache.
- You think your arm may be broken.
- You've got toothache.
- You've got a sore throat.

A: I've got a headache. What should I do?
B: You should rest.

FAST FINISHER

How many words can you make from the letters in the word *toothache*?

the, hot, ...

LS Language summary: Unit 5 SB p. 131

KEEP TALKING!

What should I do?

READING and LISTENING

I can understand an advice forum.

1 Work in pairs. Who do you talk to when you've got a problem: your parents, your friends or someone else?

2 Read *Today's posts* on the *TeenHelp* advice forum. Complete the summary of the problems with words from each post.

1 Anya is nervous about a ... to her ... .

2 Sammy always feels ... when he's at ... .

3 Rochelle is worried about a ... . Some boys are ... him.

3 Read the expert's advice on the *TeenHelp* advice forum. Match each problem with two pieces of advice.

TEENHELP

Search

HOME | GET ADVICE | BLOG | REGISTER

TODAY'S POSTS

Have you got a problem? Get advice from our experts. No problem is too big or too small.

Write or Call

1 @Anya_14
I'm giving a presentation to my class next week, but I'm really nervous. Every time I think about it, my hands start to sweat, and my heart beats really fast. What should I do?

2 @Sammy_123
I'm always tired at school. Sometimes I can't sleep and then it's really hard to concentrate in class. On Saturdays and Sundays I just want to stay in bed all morning.

3 @Rochelle
Some boys at school are bullying one of my classmates. He doesn't want to tell anyone because he's worried it will make things worse. But he's really upset about it.

OUR EXPERT'S ADVICE

a Teenagers need a lot of sleep because their bodies and brains are growing. You should avoid going to bed too late, and make sure you're getting the eight or nine hours of sleep that you need.

b If it's happening at school, you should help your friend to tell a teacher, or talk to the teacher yourself. Adults need to know when bad things happen so that they can help.

c Practise the night before, and write important words and phrases on cards. Don't try and learn the whole speech because if you forget it, you'll probably panic.

d Show him that you're a friend. For example, if you walk with him to school or sit with him at lunch, he won't feel so alone. Friends can make a big difference.

e You should take a bottle of water with you on the day because your mouth may get dry. Smile, speak slowly, and don't forget to breathe! Good luck!

f Getting up late at the weekend isn't the answer. You should get some exercise during the day. It will make it easier for you to go to sleep, and you won't feel so tired the next day.

4 Work in pairs. Do you agree with the advice for each problem? What other advice do you have?

5 5.9 Listen to the phone call to *TeenHelp*. What is the boy's problem?

6 5.9 Listen again. What is Janet's advice? Do you agree with it?

SPEAKING Giving advice

I can give advice about a problem.

1 5.10 **Listen and read. What is Jude's problem?**

Lucy: What's the matter, Jude? You don't look very well.
Jude: I've got a really bad stomach ache.
Lucy: Poor you. Maybe you should go home.
Jude: I can't go home. I've got an exam this afternoon.
Lucy: Yes, but you shouldn't do the exam if you've got a stomach ache.
Jude: I suppose you're right. What do you think I should do then?
Lucy: Why don't you talk to your teacher and ask if you can take the exam another day? Now what's wrong?
Jude: Mmm, I'm not sure Miss Wilson will believe me.
Lucy: I'll come with you if you want.
Jude: Thanks Lucy.
Lucy: No problem. I'm sure it'll be OK.

2 5.11 **Listen and repeat the Useful language.**

Useful language

Expressing concern
What's the matter?
What's wrong?
You don't look very well/happy.

Giving advice
Maybe you should ...
You shouldn't ...
Why don't you ...?
I'm sure it'll be OK.

3 5.12 **Put the dialogue in order. Listen and check.**

a **Nathan:** I think you should tell her you're sorry.
b **Julia:** Yes, but she doesn't want to talk to me.
c **Nathan:** Don't worry, I'm sure everything will be OK.
d **Julia:** I suppose you're right.
e **Nathan:** Doesn't she? Oh, maybe you should send her a message.
f **Julia:** I had an argument with my best friend and I said some horrible things to her. What do you think I should do?
g **Nathan:** What's wrong, Julia? You look upset.

4 Work in pairs. Give advice to a friend about his/her problem. Follow the steps in the Speaking plan.

Speaking plan

Prepare
- Choose one of the situations below. Decide what the problem is.
  - You don't understand one of your school lessons.
  - Someone at school stole something of yours.
  - You're stressed about something and you can't sleep.
- Think of advice and make notes for your dialogue.

Speak
- Practise your dialogue.
- Use phrases from the **Useful language** box.
- Act out your dialogue without notes.

Reflect
- How can you improve next time?
- Swap roles and choose a new situation.

Now play *Keep moving!*

FAST FINISHER
Choose one of the problems on page 54 or 55. Write more advice for the problem.

LS Language summary: Unit 5 SB p. 131

REAL CULTURE!

Vegan Britain

I can compare alternative diets in the UK with diets in my own country.

THE VEGAN REVOLUTION

More and more people in the UK are giving up meat. A recent survey found that 10% of British children aged eight to sixteen are vegan or vegetarian, and 44% are trying to eat less meat.

WHAT IS A VEGAN?

A vegan is someone who doesn't eat any animal products, such as meat, fish, eggs, dairy* products, and even honey. Some people call this 'a plant-based diet'. A lot of vegans also don't wear clothes that are made from animal products, for example, leather shoes or jackets.

*dairy = made from milk

MEAT-FREE MONDAYS

Some schools in the UK have 'Meat-free Mondays' when, one day a week, they only serve vegetarian or vegan lunches, for example, spicy bean tacos, spinach and potato curry, or nut burgers.

'The food tastes great, and at the same time we're caring for our planet and environment.'
Beth, 14

WHY ARE SO MANY TEENS BECOMING VEGAN?

Hannah, 15

I became vegan because I care about animals and don't agree with eating them. I also want to help the planet. The production of meat creates a lot of pollution and carbon dioxide, and is one of the main causes of climate change.

Benja, 16

I wanted to eat more healthily and lose weight. Fruit and vegetables are full of vitamins and minerals, but you should always plan your meals carefully to make sure you get everything your body needs, including protein.

FAMOUS VEGANS

A lot of famous people are vegan. British world champion Formula 1 driver Lewis Hamilton decided to stop eating meat to help the environment and improve his health. Other famous vegans include the tennis champion, Novak Djokovic, and the singer, Ariana Grande.

1 **Work in pairs. What is a vegan? Which of these things do vegans eat? Which don't they eat?**

beans cheese eggs fish honey meat milk nuts pineapple spinach

2 5.13 **Read and listen to the article and check your answers to Exercise 1.**

3 **Read the article again. Are the sentences true (T) or false (F)? Correct the false sentences.**

1. One in ten children in Britain aged eight to sixteen are vegan or vegetarian.
2. You can eat eggs in a plant-based diet.
3. Hannah says that a vegan diet is bad for the planet.
4. Benja became vegan because he wanted to protect animals.
5. Vegans have to be careful to eat all the vitamins their body needs.
6. Some schools don't serve meat one day a week.
7. Beth doesn't like the food at school.
8. Lewis Hamilton became vegan to be healthier and protect the planet.

4 **Word Power** **Copy and complete the table. Find the missing food groups in the article. Which food groups should we eat most of to be healthy?**

Food groups	Examples
1 ...	meat, fish, nuts
2 ...	milk, yoghurt, ice cream
3 ...	apples, broccoli, tomatoes
4 carbohydrates	bread, rice, pasta
5 fats and sugars	butter, chocolate, oil

5 **Read the interview about Veganuary and answer the questions.**

1. What and when is Veganuary?
2. Which food groups in Exercise 4 does Max like most?
3. Do you think he'll complete the challenge. Why/Why not?

6 5.14 **Listen to Max's podcast. Who did he do the challenge with? Did he complete it?**

7 5.14 **Listen again and answer the questions.**

1. What does Max think at the start of the challenge?
2. Why does he say 'It's not fair' on Day 2 of the challenge?
3. How did Max's friends react?
4. How does Max feel at the end of the challenge? Give examples.
5. Does Max think he will continue with his vegan diet? Why/Why not?

8 **COMPARE CULTURES** **Discuss the questions in small groups.**

1. Do people eat a lot of meat in your country?
2. Are vegan or vegetarian diets popular?
3. Could you do the Veganuary challenge? Why/Why not?

9 **GET CREATIVE** **Work in small groups. Imagine you're having a vegan day. Plan your meals: breakfast, lunch and dinner. Remember: no meat, fish, eggs or dairy products!**

Now watch the culture video.

FAST FINISHER
Imagine you're doing the Veganuary challenge. Answer the questions in the interview with Max.

Veganuary challenge

Veganuary is a charity that encourages people to go vegan for the month of January. We challenged fourteen-year-old Max to try it. Before he started, we asked him a few questions:

Do you eat a lot of meat?
Yes, I do. I love meat, especially chicken and lamb.

Do you eat a lot of dairy products?
I eat a lot of cheese, and I always have cereal with milk for breakfast.

What food will you miss the most during the challenge?
I think I'll miss fried chicken, my dad's cheesecake, pizza, and I love pasta, too ... loads of things!

Do you like vegetables?
I don't mind broccoli or sweetcorn, but I don't eat a lot of vegetables.

Do you think you'll feel healthier at the end of the month?
I don't know. I think protein is good for my bones and muscles ... without meat it might be difficult!

Stay safe

WRITING A *How to* ... guide

I can write a *How to ...* guide.

1 Read the title of the blog post. What's your advice for staying safe online? Discuss your ideas as a class.

2 Read the blog post. What advice does it give? Does it mention any of your ideas from Exercise 1?

The internet is a great way to connect with friends and have fun, but there are dangers, too. Here are our top tips for staying safe online.

1 ...

It's important not to give any personal information online, such as your phone number or the name of your school. On social media, you should always check your privacy settings so that only friends can see your posts.

2 ...

It's a good idea to only play or chat with people you know in real life. If someone you don't know asks to be your friend, don't accept their request – people aren't always who they say they are. Never meet with someone that you only know online.

3 ...

Be careful with any photos or videos that you post, especially if they're a bit embarrassing. Remember that other people can share your photos, and then they're out of your control. If you're writing a post on social media, always show respect. You may not agree with someone, but you should never be rude.

3 Read the blog post again and match the headings with the paragraphs. There is one extra heading.

a Be careful who your 'friends' are
b Think about what you put online
c Choose a password that you won't forget
d Protect your identity and privacy

4 Look at the **Useful language**. How do you say these expressions in your language?

Useful language

Giving tips and advice

Here are (my) top tips for ...
It's important (not) to ...
You should always/never ...
It's a good idea to ...
Remember that ...

5 Study the **Look!** box. How do we make affirmative and negative sentences with imperatives?

Look! Imperatives

We usually use imperatives to give instructions.
***Think** about what you put online.*
***Don't accept** their request.*
We can use ***always*** and ***never*** with imperatives.
***Always show** respect.*
***Never meet** with someone that you only know online.*

6 Complete the advice with affirmative or negative imperatives. Use the verbs in the box.

choose	give	put	speak	spend

1 ... passwords that other people can't guess.
2 ... anything online that you wouldn't like your parents to see.
3 Never ... your passwords to anyone.
4 ... all your free time online.
5 ... to an adult if you're worried about anything.

7 Write a ***How to ...*** guide. Follow the steps in the **Writing plan**.

Writing plan

Prepare

› Choose your topic:
  - How to stay healthy
  - How to do well in your exa
› Make notes about your tips and advice. What should yo do? What shouldn't you do?
› Group your ideas under headings, for example, *Before t exam, On the day of the exam, ...*

Write

› Organize your ideas into paragraphs:
  - Introduction.
  - Use a different paragraph for each heading.
  - Use the expressions from the **Useful language** box.

Check

› Check your grammar: *should* and *shouldn't*.
› Check imperatives and your spelling.

Special days

6

Vocabulary: Party plans; Things for a camping trip **Grammar:** *be going to* and *will*; Future arrangements; Reflexive pronouns **Speaking:** Asking for and offering help **Writing:** A thank-you letter

VOCABULARY Party plans

I can talk about plans for a party.

1 6.1 **Copy and complete the party guide with the words in the box. Listen, check and repeat.**

date decorations DJ fun guest list invitations lights place playlist snacks social media takeaway

2 **What makes a good party? Put these things in order of importance. Then compare in pairs.**

- a good playlist or DJ
- food and snacks
- guests
- place
- lights and decorations
- other things (your ideas)

3 **Work in pairs. Did you have a party for your last birthday? What did you do?**

A: For my last birthday, I had an ice-skating party!
B: Wow! That sounds amazing.

4 PRONUNCIATION /ʃ/

6.2 **Listen and repeat. Pay attention to the /ʃ/ sound.**

decorations invitation social media

5 6.3 **Practise saying these words. Listen, check and repeat.**

celebration machine Russian show special sugar

6 **Complete the sentences with the correct verb from Exercise 1.**

My sister is going to be fifteen next month. She wants to throw the perfect party – and I'm helping her to plan it! I told her to [1] … a date and to [2] … a guest list. She wants to [3] … the invitations by email. Mum says it's too expensive to [4] … a takeaway or [5] … a DJ, so we are going to [6] … some snacks and [7] … a playlist – and [8] … some decorations, of course! We have two party rules:
1 Don't [9] … photos on social media!
2 [10] … fun!

Now watch the vlog.

FAST FINISHER

Imagine your dream party. Where are you? What is everybody doing? What food is there?

LS Language summary: Unit 6 SB p. 132

Birthday celebrations

READING

I can scan a web page for specific information.

1 **Work in pairs. How old will you be on your next birthday? How do you want to celebrate it?**

2 **Scan the survey quickly. Find answers to these questions.**

1 In total, how many people wrote comments?
2 Of the three people here, who is the youngest person to write a comment?
3 Apart from surveys, what other things can you find on this website?
4 What time did Theo write his comment?

COOLTEENS.uk

Film News | Science & Technology | Style | Surveys | Fun & Games

Survey: Your Birthday

Everybody likes to celebrate their birthday differently. Perhaps you like big parties with lots of friends, or maybe you prefer simple celebrations at home with your family. If your birthday's in winter, you probably won't have a barbecue or a beach party, and if you have a summer birthday, you definitely won't go ice-skating in the park! So, how are you going to celebrate your next birthday? Write and tell us!

67 comments

Jordan, 15 *21 March at 11.13*

My birthday's in November. I'm going to have a karaoke party, with about five of my friends. My dad's going to hire a karaoke machine, and we're all going to sing our favourite songs. I want to find some cheap wigs and sunglasses so that people can dress up as their favourite singer! I'm sure we'll have lots of fun!

Hayley, 13 *21 March at 11.37*

My birthday's in July. I'm possibly going to go to a theme park – if my parents agree. I love theme parks and I really want to go on Nemesis – it's a really fast and scary rollercoaster. I'll probably feel sick afterwards, but I'll definitely go on it again – straight away!

Theo, 14 *21 March at 12.05*

I'm fifteen next month. I'm not going to have a big party, I'm just going to have a small celebration with my parents, aunts, uncles and cousins. There'll probably be about twelve or thirteen people. My mum's going to make pizzas and we're going to play games outside. Hopefully it won't rain!

Show more comments

3 6.4 **Read and listen to the survey and answer the questions.**

1 Who wants to have a party with a few friends?
2 Who wants to have a party with music?
3 Who wants to have a party with family?
4 Who wants the weather to be nice?
5 Who doesn't want to celebrate at home?

4 **Word Power** **Look at the examples of adverbs of certainty. Find three more adverbs of certainty in the survey.**

Perhaps you like big parties.
You **probably** won't have a barbecue.

5 **FIND OUT** **How many people in the world are celebrating a birthday today?**

GRAMMAR *be going to*

I can talk about future plans.

Now watch the grammar animation.

1 **Read the grammar box. What form of the main verb do we use after *be going to*?**

Affirmative

I'**m going to have** a karaoke party.
My dad'**s going to hire** a karaoke machine.
We'**re going to sing** our favourite songs.

Negative

I'**m not going to have** a big party.
He **isn't going to invite** any friends.
They **aren't going to play** games.

Questions	Short answers
Is she **going to make** pizzas?	Yes, she **is**. / No, she **isn't**.

2 **Anna and Liam are each planning a party. Look at the list and complete sentences 1–6.**

PARTY PLANS

	Anna	Liam
invite a lot of guests	✓	✗
buy snacks	✓	✗
order a takeaway	✗	✓
create a playlist	✓	✗
put up decorations	✓	✓
hire a DJ	✗	✗

Liam *isn't going to invite* a lot of guests.
1 Anna … snacks.
2 Liam … snacks.
3 Liam … a takeaway.
4 Anna … a playlist.
5 They … decorations.
6 They … a DJ.

3 **How are you going to celebrate your next birthday? Write sentences. Use the suggestions below and your own ideas.**

I'm going to go to a bowling alley.
I'm not going to invite a lot of guests.

- Place
- Number of guests
- Food and drink
- Music
- Decorations

4 **Work in pairs. Ask and answer about your plans.**

Where are you going to celebrate your next birthday?

I'm going to invite a few friends to come to my flat. What about you?

be going to and *will*

I can talk about future plans and predictions.

5 **Look at the grammar box. Copy and complete the rules with *be going to* and *will*.**

I'**m going to have** a small celebration.
There'**ll** probably **be** about twelve or thirteen people.
We'**re going to play** games outside.
Hopefully it **won't rain**!

Rules

We use [1] … to make predictions about the future.
We use [2] … to talk about future plans and intentions.

6 **Complete Chloe's comment with *be going to* or *will* and the verbs in brackets.**

Chloe, 13 *21 March at 12.19*

It's my fourteenth birthday next Saturday. I [1] … (get up) early and have a birthday breakfast with my family. I hope there [2] … (be) some presents and cards to open! In the afternoon, I [3] … (have) a small party with my classmates. We [4] … (go) ice-skating. Some of my friends don't know how to skate, but I'm sure they [5] … (learn) quickly, and hopefully there [6] … (not be) any accidents! Afterwards, we [7] … (eat) at my favourite Italian restaurant. I'm sure everybody [8] … (be) really hungry.

7 **Make questions with *be going to* or *will*. Ask and answer in pairs.**

What (you / have) for dinner tonight?
A: What are you going to have for dinner tonight?
B: I'm probably going to have spaghetti.

1 What (mobile phones / be like) in the future?
2 (you / watch) a film tonight?
3 In the future, (humans / build) homes on other planets?
4 When (you / do) your homework?
5 (drones / deliver) our food in future?

FUN FACT

In the UK, if you reach your 100th birthday, the king or queen sends you a birthday card!

FAST FINISHER

Write about your plans and predictions for the summer.

We're going to go to France. Dad will probably get sunburn on the beach!

LS Language summary: Unit 6 SB p. 132

A music festival

VOCABULARY and LISTENING Things for a camping trip

I can listen for specific information in a phone call.

1 **Are music festivals popular in your country? Have you ever been to one? Discuss the questions as a class.**

2 6.5 **Match the words in the box with the pictures. Listen, check and repeat.**

first-aid kit	hoodie	phone charger	pillow
raincoat	sleeping bag	soap	sun cream
sunglasses	tent	toothbrush	torch
towel	water bottle		

3 **Complete the blog with objects from Exercise 2.**

Are you going to a music festival this summer? We want you and your friends to enjoy yourselves, so here are our top tips!

- If it's sunny, you'll need some [1] … and a pair of [2] … .
- It can get cold in the evening, so make sure you take a [3] … to wear.
- It may rain – it is the UK after all! – so take a [4] … .
- If it rains, you'll want to dry yourself, so pack a [5] … .
- It's a good idea to take a [6] … in case you cut yourself.

4 **In pairs, imagine you're going on a camping trip this weekend. Think about the weather, and agree what you will need to take with you.**

A: It's going to rain this weekend. We'll need to take our raincoats.

B: And we'll need a tent, of course!

5 6.6 **Lucy phones her friend Seb to invite him to a festival. Listen and answer the questions.**

1 When is the festival?
2 Apart from Lucy and her dad, who else is going?
3 Where are they staying?
4 What does Seb need to do before he buys his ticket?

6 6.6 **Copy Seb's notes. Listen again and complete them.**

Name of festival:	Big Green Music Festival
Date of festival:	*5th and 6th May*
Price of ticket:	[1] …
Things to take:	[2] … , torch, [3] …
Transport:	[4] …
Day/time of leaving:	[5] … at [6] … a.m.

LS Language summary: Unit 6 SB p. 132

GRAMMAR Present continuous for future arrangements

I can talk about future arrangements.

Now watch the grammar animation.

1 **Read the grammar box. Copy and complete the rules with *future*, *present* and *weekend*.**

Are you **doing** anything next weekend?
I'**m going** to the Big Green Music Festival.
How **are** you **getting** there?
Dad'**s driving**. We'**re leaving** on Saturday morning at 9.00.

Rules

We can use the [1] ... continuous to talk about arrangements (fixed plans) in the [2] ... .

We often use a time expression, for example, *tomorrow*, *next* [3] ... , *on Saturday*.

2 6.7 **Complete the dialogue using the present continuous. Which actions refer to the future? Which actions are happening now? Listen and check.**

Seb: Hi, Lucy. I spoke to my mum, and – guess what? I [1] ... (come) to the festival next weekend!
Lucy: That's great news. Oh, there's a small change to the plan. Dad [2] ... (not drive) because there's a problem with the car. We [3] ... (get) the bus instead. We [4] ... (leave) here at 8.30.
Seb: That's fine. [5] ... (you / take) any food with you?
Lucy: Just a few snacks. I [6] ... (pack) them right now. We can buy food at the campsite.
Seb: OK, and what [7] ... (you / wear) on Saturday?
Lucy: I [8] ... (wear) shorts and a T-shirt.
Seb: Great. I [9] ... (feel) really excited! See you on Saturday morning.

3 **Work in pairs. Ask and answer questions about your plans. Use the ideas in the box.**

A: What are you doing after school?
B: I'm playing football in the park with a few friends. What about you?

What Who Where	do meet go	after school? tomorrow? next weekend?

Reflexive pronouns

I can use reflexive pronouns.

4 **Read the grammar box and the rule. Choose the correct answer.**

Reflexive pronouns

I fixed my bike **myself**.
Did **you** hurt **yourself** when you fell?
Joe cut **himself** with a knife.
She really enjoyed **herself** at the concert.
We taught **ourselves** to play the guitar.
Did **you** make the invitations **yourselves**?
They introduced **themselves** to their new teacher.

Rule

We use a reflexive pronoun when [1] *the same / a different* person is the subject and the object of a verb.

5 **Complete the sentences with the correct reflexive pronoun.**

1 We really enjoyed ... at the music festival.
2 He fell off his bike and hurt ... .
3 I'm teaching ... Japanese. It's really hard!
4 Don't go too close to the fire, children! You'll burn ... .
5 I gave her a towel so that she could dry ... .
6 They introduced ... to everybody at the party.
7 The whale cut ... on some rocks.
8 Sally, are you talking to ... ?

6 **Write sentences about you and your family and friends. Use the verbs in the box and a reflexive pronoun.**

cut enjoy hurt talk to teach

My dad cut himself on some glass last week.
My sister is teaching herself coding.

FAST FINISHER

Imagine you're going to a festival at the weekend. Where is it? Who is going with you? What's happening there? What are you taking?

I'm going to a festival. I'm going with ...

LS Language summary: Unit 6 SB p. 132

KEEP TALKING!

A special occasion

READING and LISTENING

I can understand messages in a variety of greetings cards.

1 **Work in pairs. Do you give birthday cards to your friends or family? On what other occasions do you usually give cards?**

2 **Match the occasions in the box with the cards. There are two extra occasions.**

Birthday   Christmas   Mother's Day   Moving to a new school
New Year   Passing your exams   Wedding

a

b

c

d

e

3 **Match the cards with the messages inside them.**

1

Thanks for everything you do for me. I may not be the perfect son, but you're definitely the perfect mum!

Love

Jordan

2

Dear Amy

Another year older – we can't believe it! Have a great day and a fun party tonight!

Lots of love

Mum and Dad

3

To Joseph

Thanks for being a great friend and classmate. Hope you make lots of friends at your new place!

We'll miss you! Good luck!

Everybody in Class 8B

4

To Camila

Wishing you peace and happiness this holiday season. Hope Father Christmas brings you lots of lovely presents!

See you in the New Year!

Becky x

5

To our amazing, hard-working Emma

Congratulations! We knew you could do it! You're a star!

Lots of love

Auntie Vicky and Uncle Bob

4 **Read the cards and messages again and answer the questions.**

1 How is Amy celebrating her birthday?
2 Who is moving to a new school?
3 Is Jordan a boy or a girl?
4 Who sent a card to their niece?
5 What are two names for the person who brings the presents at Christmas?

5 **6.8 Listen. What is the occasion in each dialogue?**

6 **6.8 Listen again and answer the questions.**

Dialogue 1

1 Where is Susie?
2 What did her brother buy for their mum?

Dialogue 2

3 Why is Felix leaving?
4 What is he doing this afternoon?

Dialogue 3

5 What was Chloe's Maths result?
6 What is she doing tonight to celebrate?

7 **GET CREATIVE** **Work in small groups. Choose an occasion from Exercise 2. Design a greetings card and write a message inside the card. As a class, vote for the best card.**

SPEAKING Asking for and offering help

I can ask for and offer help.

1 6.9 **Listen and read. Match the dialogue with one of the messages on page 64.**

Amy: Hello?
Zac: Hi, Amy, it's Zac! Shall I help you get ready for the party tonight? I could come over after lunch?
Amy: Yes please, that would be really helpful.
Zac: So, what can I do to help?
Amy: Could you make the sandwiches?
Zac: No problem. Cheese and tomato?
Amy: Perfect!
Zac: Do you want me to cook the pizzas, too?
Amy: That would be great. And after that, would you mind creating a playlist?
Zac: Sure. I'll put on lots of party songs that everybody knows.
Amy: Great. While you're doing that, I'll go to the shop and buy the drinks. And then I think we'll be ready!
Zac: Great. I can't wait for the party!

2 Read the dialogue again. Which jobs is Zac going to do?

3 6.10 **Listen and repeat the Useful language.**

Useful language

Asking for help
Could you ...?
Would you mind ...?

Offering help
Shall I help you ...?
What can I do to help?
Do you want me to ...?
I'll ...

Accepting help
That would be great/really helpful.

4 6.11 **Put the dialogue in the correct order. Listen and check.**

a **Maya:** No problem. We could play musical chairs!
b **Dad:** That would be great. Then, could you plan some games?
c **Maya:** This is going to be a great party – Mum will love it!
d **Dad:** Thanks, Maya. Would you mind making a guest list? Just family and neighbours.
e **Maya:** Do you want me to help you plan Mum's surprise birthday party?
f **Dad:** Brilliant idea. Everybody loves that game!
g **Maya:** Sure. Shall I send the invitations, too?

5 Work in pairs. Ask for and offer help in one of the situations below. Follow the steps in the Speaking plan.

Your friend needs some help to tidy up after a party. These are some of the jobs:
- tidy the living room
- do the washing up
- clean the kitchen
- take out the rubbish

Your friend needs some help to organize a barbecue. These are some of the jobs:
- light the barbecue
- cook the burgers
- make a salad
- plan some games

Speaking plan

Prepare
- Decide on your roles.
- Make notes for your dialogue.

Speak
- Practise your dialogue.
- Use phrases from the **Useful language** box.
- Act out your dialogue without notes.

Reflect
- How can you improve next time?
- Swap roles and choose a new situation.

Now play *Keep moving!*

FAST FINISHER
Imagine that your class is organizing a party for the end of term. Write a list of the jobs, like the lists in Exercise 5.

LS Language summary: Unit 6 SB p. 132

EXPLORE CULTURE!

Happy New Year!

I can compare New Year and winter celebrations in the UK with celebrations in my country.

SEARCH LOG IN

ComeToBritain.com

PLACES TO GO | THINGS TO DO | BLOG | SHOP

New Year celebrations in the UK

How do you usually celebrate New Year? In the UK, there are lots of interesting celebrations at the end of an old year and the start of a new one. Here are our three top suggestions.

1 New Year, London

Many cities and towns in the UK celebrate New Year with firework shows. One of the biggest and most famous is in London. At midnight on New Year's Eve, Big Ben rings twelve times to welcome the New Year, and the fireworks begin. Thousands of people stand along the River Thames to watch the show. Then, on New Year's Day, there is a big parade through the streets with carnival dancers, marching bands, magicians and giant balloons!

2 Hogmanay, Edinburgh

The Scottish name for the New Year celebrations is Hogmanay. In Edinburgh, Hogmanay starts on 30 December with a big parade. Then, on New Year's Eve, there is a huge street party with musicians, acrobats and fire eaters. At midnight, there is an amazing firework show over Edinburgh Castle. People hold hands and sing the traditional song Auld Lang Syne. The celebrations don't stop there! On New Year's Day, people dress up in funny costumes and dive into the freezing cold River Forth!

3 Up Helly Aa, Shetland Islands

Up Helly Aa is a festival that takes place on the Shetland Islands in Scotland. It happens later in January. People dress up as Vikings wearing helmets, and walk through the streets carrying torches of fire. They pull a full-size model of a Viking longship through the streets, and then, after singing the Up Helly Aa song, the parade ends when they throw their torches onto the ship. As the ship burns, the crowd sings one more song, and then everybody returns to the town for a big party!

a

b

c

d

e

f

1 **Look at the pictures on page 66. In which picture(s) can you see ...**

1 fireworks? 2 a parade? 3 costumes?

2 6.12 **Read and listen to the information on the website about three celebrations in the UK. Match the celebrations with the pictures.**

3 **Read the website again. Copy and complete the table.**

	In London ...	In Edinburgh ...	In the Shetland Islands ...
1 there is a parade.	✓	✓	✓
2 there are fireworks.			
3 there are musicians.			
4 people go swimming.			
5 people sing songs.			
6 people celebrate after 1 January.			
7 people wear costumes.			
8 people burn a boat.			

4 **Word Power** **A performer is a person who entertains an audience – for example, a singer or an actor. Find five types of performers in the text.**

5 **What are New Year's resolutions? Read the text and complete the resolutions with the words in the box.**

be do eat listen save spend start stop

OUR NEW YEAR'S RESOLUTIONS

We asked four British teenagers about their New Year's resolutions – the things they want to do or change in their lives during the next year. Here's what they said:

I want to [1] ... more healthily. I'm going to [2] ... eating junk food and chocolate.

I want to [3] ... money for my summer holiday. I'm going to get a Saturday job and [4] ... less.

I want to get better results at school. I'm going to [5] ... more in class and [6] ... more homework.

I want to [7] ... fitter. I'm going to join a dance club or [8] ... running.

6 6.13 **Listen to the two interviews. How did each person spend New Year? What are their New Year's resolutions?**

7 6.13 **Compare your answers in pairs. Listen again and check.**

8 **COMPARE CULTURES** **How do people celebrate New Year in your country? Are there any special traditions? What do you and your family usually do?**

9 **THINK CRITICALLY** **What New Year's resolutions would you like to make for next year? Think about:**

- *things you would like to change, and why*
- *new things you would like to learn, and why*
- *things you would like to start (or stop) doing, and why*

Now watch the culture video.

FAST FINISHER

Imagine you're organizing a special New Year celebration for all your family and friends. Write about your plans.

First, I'm going to have a big concert with all my favourite musicians. Then, at midnight, we're going to ...

A lovely surprise

WRITING A thank-you letter

I can write a thank-you letter.

1 Read the letter. What did Layla get for her birthday? What is she going to do next weekend?

Dear Auntie Clare and Uncle Tony

Thank you for the card and present that you sent me for my birthday. It was a lovely surprise and very kind of you. I love the headphones — they're perfect for listening to music everywhere I go!

I had a great birthday. I got up early and opened my presents before school. Then, in the evening, we ordered a Chinese takeaway — my favourite! I got some fantastic presents — money from Mum and Dad, and some earrings from Oscar. I'm thinking of using the money to buy a new bike as my old one is a bit small for me now.

Next week is the last week of term. We've got exams all week so I'm not looking forward to that! On Friday night, I'm going to a friend's house for a sleepover. We're going to watch a film and have pizza and cake! We probably won't get any sleep, but it'll be fun!

Thanks again for the brilliant present. I really appreciate it.

Lots of love

Layla

2 Look at the **Useful language**. How do you say these expressions in your language?

Useful language

Writing a thank-you letter

Dear ...
Thank you for the ... that you sent me.
It was very kind/generous of you.
I had a great/fantastic birthday.
Lots of love / Best wishes

3 Read the **Look!** box. Find one more example of a preposition + *-ing* in the letter.

Look! Preposition + *-ing*

If a verb comes after a preposition, we often use the *-ing* form of the verb.

*They're perfect **for listening** to music.*

4 Copy and complete the sentences. Use the *-ing* form of the verbs in the box.

go have make remember see

1 I'm excited about ... my friends.
3 He's good at ... cakes.
2 Are you scared of ... on the rollercoaster?
4 She's isn't keen on ... a party for her birthday.
5 Thanks for ... my birthday!

5 Write a letter to say thank you for a present. Follow the steps in the **Writing plan**.

Writing plan

Prepare

› Make notes for your letter. What is the present and who is it from? What do you like about it?

Write

› Organize your ideas into paragraphs:
- Thank the person for the present.
- Describe what you did on your birthday (or other special occasion).
- Describe some other news.

› Use the expressions from the **Useful language** box.

Check

› Check your grammar: *be going to*, *will* and present continuous.

› Check prepositions + *-ing* and your spelling.

W **Writing summary** WB p. 89
R **Review: Units 4–6** SB pp. 102–103
P **Project: Units 4–6** SB pp. 108–109
L **Literature: Units 4–6** SB pp. 114–115
E **Exams: Unit 6** SB p. 123
LS **Language summary: Unit 6** SB p. 132

7 Amazing adventures

Vocabulary: Expressions with *get, go, make* and *take*; Feelings | **Grammar:** Present perfect affirmative, negative and questions; *ever* and *never* | **Speaking:** Asking for information | **Writing:** A blog post

VOCABULARY Expressions with *get, go, make* and *take*

I can talk about experiences I'd like to have.

1 What's a bucket list? Read and check. Complete Joseph's list with the verbs in the box.

get (x3) | go (x2) | make (x2) | take (x2)

2 7.1 Listen, check and repeat the answers to Exercise 1. Which of the activities would you most like to do?

3 Work in pairs. Ask and answer the questions.

1. What would you like to get better at?
2. Do you sometimes take part in competitions or events? Where?
3. Where would you most like to go on an adventure?
4. What other activities from Joseph's bucket list would you like to do?

4 Copy and complete the table with the words in blue from Exercise 1. Add the words from the box below. Can you think of any more?

abroad | a break | a photo | a suggestion | married | on holiday | plans | ready | rock climbing

get	go	make	take
	scuba diving		

Now watch the vlog.

FAST FINISHER

What's on your bucket list? Write sentences.

LS Language summary: Unit 7 SB p. 133

Pushing your limits

READING

I can understand paraphrased sentences.

1 **Look at the pictures. What part of the world do you think they show? What are some of the dangers there?**

2 7.2 **Read and listen to the article. Check your answers to Exercise 1.**

JOURNEY TO THE ENDS OF THE EARTH

Jade Hameister is still a teenager, but she's done more in her life than most people do in their lifetime. She's skied to the North Pole, she's crossed glaciers in Greenland, and she's trekked to the South Pole. She's broken world records and is the youngest person in history to reach both poles.

It hasn't been easy. To prepare for her travels, Jade – from Melbourne in Australia – trained for hours after school and at weekends. During her adventures, she faced temperatures of -40°C. Other dangers included polar bears and the risk of falling through thin ice into freezing water. Altogether, she travelled 1,300 km. She skied for eight to ten hours every day, and pulled a huge 50 kg sledge behind her.

During her 37-day journey to the South Pole, an exhausted Jade wrote, 'I've lost the feeling in my fingers and toes and my body aches everywhere … It has been 26 days since my last shower. I would do anything for a bath and a home-cooked meal (even just a piece of toast!).'

Jade has given talks and written a book about her experiences. She feels strongly about what climate change is doing to the Arctic and Antarctic. Average temperatures there have increased by a terrifying 2–3°C in the last 50 years, and that affects humans and animals everywhere on Earth. Jade also wants to inspire other young people to follow their dreams and push their limits. 'If you have a dream, just get started,' she says.

JADE'S RECORD-BREAKING JOURNEYS

1 **North Pole**
Distance: 150 km
Length: 11 days
Record: Youngest person in history (age 14)

2 **Greenland crossing**
Distance: 550 km
Length: 27 days
Record: Youngest woman in history (age 15)

3 **South Pole**
Distance: 600 km
Length: 37 days
Record: Youngest person in history (age 16)

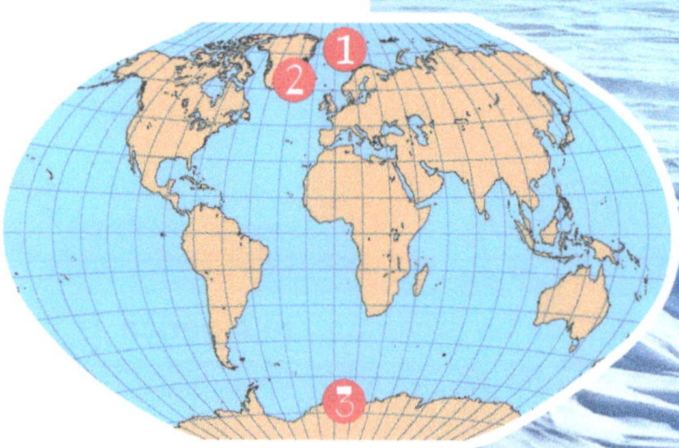

3 **Read the article again. Copy and complete the sentences with one, two or three words from the text.**

Jade is the youngest person to go to the North and *South* poles.

1 Jade … hard for her journeys in her free time.
2 Polar bears were just one of the … on her trip.
3 Jade couldn't feel her … as she trekked through Antarctica.
4 She really wanted some hot food and … .
5 The Arctic and Antarctic are getting warmer because of … .
6 Jade would like to help young people's … come true.

4 **Word Power** **Match the extreme adjectives in blue in the text with the definitions.**

1 very big
2 very tired
3 very cold
4 very scary

5 **THINK CRITICALLY** **Work in pairs and discuss. Why do people go on extreme and dangerous expeditions?**

6 **FIND OUT** **Who was the first person to reach the South Pole? When was it, and where was he from?**

GRAMMAR Present perfect affirmative and negative

I can talk about experiences in my life.

Now watch the grammar animation.

1 **Read the grammar box. Choose the correct answer to complete the rules.**

Affirmative

I**'ve skied** to the North Pole.
He/She**'s written** a book.
We/You/They**'ve broken** a world record.

Negative

I **haven't crossed** glaciers.
He/She **hasn't seen** a polar bear.
We/You/They **haven't been** to the South Pole.

Rules

We use the present perfect to describe an experience in someone's life. We [1] *say / don't say* exactly when the experience happened.

We form the present perfect with the correct form of [2] *have / be* + past participle.

To form the past participle of [3] *regular / irregular* verbs, we add *-ed* to the verb.

2 **Write the past participles of these verbs. Use the Irregular verbs list on page 136 to help you.**

climb eat have meet ride see
sleep study travel win

3 **Copy and complete the sentences about Jade's family. Use the present perfect affirmative.**

1 Jade's dad is a mountaineer. He ... some of the world's highest mountains. (climb)
2 Jade ... at Everest base camp. (sleep)
3 Jade and her family ... around the world. (travel)
4 They ... some exciting holidays together. (have)
5 Jade ... lots of awards. (win)
6 She ... Prince Harry. (meet)

4 **Write sentences using the present perfect affirmative and negative.**

we / live in Chile ✓ in Peru ✗
We've lived in Chile, but we haven't lived in Peru.

1 I / ride a horse ✓ a camel ✗
2 my brother / eat snails ✓ insects ✗
3 they / meet Margot Robbie ✓ Emma Watson ✗
4 we / sleep in a caravan ✓ a tent ✗
5 you / win a silver medal ✓ a gold medal ✗
6 my sister / see a whale ✓ a shark ✗

5 7.3 **Complete the paragraph. Use the verbs in the box and the correct form of the present perfect. Listen and check.**

answer ask not reply not send reach
send take write

Writing to the World

When Toby Little was five, he wanted to send a letter to every country in the world. He is now a teenager, and he [1] ... his goal! Toby [2] ... to schools in China, scientists in Antarctica and wildlife rangers in Africa. He [3] ... people about their jobs, the food that they eat and their hobbies. Sadly for Toby, some people [4] ... , but a lot of people [5] ... him letters. They [6] ... Toby's questions about their country, and some people [7] ... photos to show him how they live. But there's one place that Toby [8] ... a letter to. Where is it? The Moon!

6 **Work in pairs. Talk about what you have done in your lives. Use the ideas below and your own ideas.**

eat Chinese food
hike through a forest
take part in a school play
live abroad
ride a horse
sing on stage
sleep in a tent
swim in the sea

A: I've eaten Japanese food, but I haven't eaten Chinese food.
B: I've lived in Germany. We went there when I was three.

FUN FACT

Polar bears have a powerful sense of smell. They can smell a seal from 32 km away.

FAST FINISHER

Write about more experiences you or your family have had.

My aunt has been on TV.

LS Language summary: Unit 7 SB p. 133

Have you ever felt scared?

VOCABULARY and LISTENING Feelings

I can predict answers to questions, and then listen to check.

1 7.4 **Listen and repeat the words in the box. Look at the pictures. How do you think the people are feeling? Why?**

I think he's scared because he's watching a horror film.

angry bored calm cheerful confident disappointed embarrassed excited nervous pleased scared surprised upset worried

1

2

3

4

5

6

2 Work in pairs. Copy and complete the table with the adjectives from Exercise 1. Which adjective can be both positive and negative?

Positive	Negative
calm	*angry*

3 Choose three or four of the adjectives and think about what makes you feel that way. Tell your partner, but don't say the adjective. Can they guess it?

A: I feel like this when my football team loses.

B: Disappointed?

4 Read the radio guide and look at the picture. What is a stunt actor?

7.30 p.m. Radio 7

NO FEAR Damien Green has worked as a stunt actor on some of the biggest action films. We talk to him about his exciting, but dangerous, job!

5 7.5 **Look at sentences 1–5. Which of them do you think are true about Damien and which are false? Listen and check.**

1 He's parachuted into the ocean.
2 He's jumped from a tall building.
3 He's felt scared.
4 He's worked with lots of famous actors.
5 He's been in superhero films.

6 7.5 **Listen again and answer the questions.**

1 Why was the stunt in Damien's most recent film dangerous?
2 How does he stop himself feeling scared?
3 What injuries has he had?
4 What did he do before he was a stunt actor?
5 How did he feel when he won a silver medal?
6 What would he like to do in the future?

LS Language summary: Unit 7 SB p. 133

GRAMMAR Present perfect questions; *ever* and *never*

I can ask questions about other people's experiences.

Now watch the grammar animation.

1 Read the grammar box. How do we form present perfect questions?

Questions	Short answers
Have you **dived** with sharks?	Yes, I **have**. / No, I **haven't**.
Has he **met** any famous actors?	Yes, he **has**. / No, he **hasn't**.

2 Look at the interviewer's notes and write questions and short answers.

Damien / work / with wild animals? ✓

A: Has Damien worked with wild animals?

B: Yes, he has.

Interview – Damien Green

1 any animals / attack him? ✗
2 he / crash / a lot of cars? ✓
3 he / fly a helicopter? ✗
4 he / climb / any mountains? ✓
5 he / break / his arm? ✗
6 his films / be successful? ✓

3 Work in pairs. Use the notes in Exercise 2 to act out the interview with Damien. Use 'you' and 'I' instead of 'he'.

Have any animals attacked you?

Yes, they have!

4 Read the Look! box. Write questions with the present perfect and *ever*.

Look! ***ever* and *never***

We often use *ever* with present perfect questions. It means 'at any time in your life'.

*Have you **ever** hurt yourself?*

We can also use *never* in affirmative sentences. It means 'at no time in your life'.

*I've **never** broken an arm or a leg.*

(climb) a mountain?
Have you ever climbed a mountain?

1 (be) scared at a theme park?
2 (feel) worried about an exam?
3 (meet) a famous person?
4 (dive) into the sea?
5 (eat) Japanese food?
6 (break) a bone?
7 (get) angry with a friend?

5 PRONUNCIATION Sentence stress

7.6 **Listen and repeat.**

A: Have you ever climbed a mountain?
B: Yes, I have.
A: Has she ever eaten Japanese food?
B: No, she hasn't.

6 7.7 **Work in pairs. Practise these questions and answers. Listen, check and repeat.**

A: Have you ever seen a snake?
B: Yes, I have.
A: Has he ever eaten insects?
B: No, he's never eaten insects.

7 Work in pairs. Ask and answer the questions from Exercise 4. Use *never* if you need to.

A: Have you ever climbed a mountain?
B: Yes, I have. What about you?
A: No, I've never climbed a mountain.

FAST FINISHER

Imagine you are interviewing a famous explorer about their travels, discoveries and experiences. Write questions with *Have you ever ...?*

LS Language summary: Unit 7 SB p. 133

KEEP TALKING!

Have you ever tried skydiving?

READING and LISTENING

I can understand information in an advert.

1

YOUFLY
Indoor skydiving centre

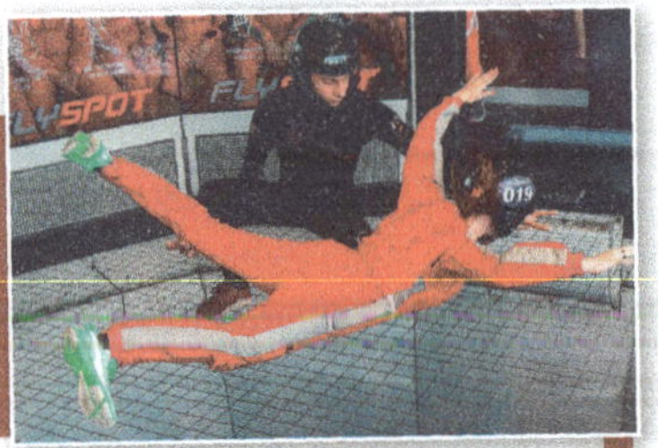

Have you ever wanted to try skydiving, but you're too scared to jump out of a plane? Then why not try indoor skydiving? Our course will teach you all you need to know.

Cost: £39.99

* *45-minute lesson with an instructor*
* *Two flights of 60 seconds each*
* *All equipment provided: flight suit, helmet and goggles*
* *DVD of your flight*

Please arrive an hour before your flight time to meet your instructor and put on your flight suit.

BOOK NOW!

2

QUAD BIKE WORLD

For an experience you'll never forget!

Prepare to drive, jump and fly through mud on our exciting quad biking course! It doesn't matter if you haven't driven before – you'll soon learn. Book now … you won't be disappointed!

~~WAS £45~~ NOW £37

* *30-minute lesson and one hour of drive time with an instructor*
* *Maximum 10 people per group*
* *Price includes hire of quad bike, helmet and protective clothing*

Additional information

Bring waterproof clothing and wear boots – you'll get very muddy!

3

BIG ROCK
REACH NEW HEIGHTS!

Have you climbed before? Do you want to go to the next level? Our four-week course is a great way to improve your rock climbing and feel more confident!

Cost: £65

What's included?

* *60 minutes a week with one of our instructors*
* *Unlimited use of our climbing wall*
* *Equipment: helmet, ropes*
* *Certificate at the end of the course*

Please bring your own climbing shoes.

CLICK HERE TO BOOK.

1 **Scan the adverts to find the name of the three sports. Which one would you most like to do? Why?**

2 **Read the adverts and answer the questions.**

1 Which course is the longest? Which course is the shortest?
2 Which course isn't for beginners?
3 Which course gives you a video?
4 For which course must you get there early?
5 For which courses must you take some of your own equipment or clothing?

3 7.8 **Listen to a dialogue between two friends, Becky and Sid. Why is Becky calling?**

4 7.8 **Listen again, and choose the correct answer, a, b or c.**

1 When do Becky and Sid decide to do the course?

a Mon Wed
b Tues Thurs
c Fri Sat

2 How much is the course?

a £70
b £65
c £45

3 What do they need to take?

a 
b 
c 

4 How are they going to get there?

a 
b 
c 

SPEAKING Asking for information

I can ask for and give information.

1 7.9 **Listen and read. Cathy is at the indoor skydiving centre. Does she book a lesson?**

Receptionist: Good morning, how can I help you?
Cathy: I'm interested in indoor skydiving.
Receptionist: Have you tried skydiving before?
Cathy: No, I haven't.
Receptionist: OK, so you'll need some lessons with our instructor.
Cathy: Do I need any special equipment?
Receptionist: No, you don't. We provide everything you need: a flight suit, a helmet and goggles.
Cathy: How much is it?
Receptionist: It's £39.99. The price includes the equipment, a lesson and two 60-second flights. You can book with me, or you can book online.
Cathy: OK, I'll get my parents to book online. Is there anything else I need to know?
Receptionist: On the day of your flight, you should get here an hour early to meet your instructor.
Cathy: Thanks very much.
Receptionist: You're welcome.

2 7.10 **Listen and repeat the Useful language.**

Useful language

Asking for and giving information

Receptionist	Customer
How can I help you?	I'm interested in ...
Have you tried ... before?	Do I need any special equipment?
We provide ...	How much is it?
The price includes ...	Is there anything else I need to know?

3 7.11 **Copy and complete the dialogue with the phrases in the box. Listen and check.**

How much is it? I'm interested in kayaking.
You should bring a towel and warm clothes
No, but you should wear old clothes – you'll get wet.

Receptionist: Hello, how can I help you?
Emma: 1 ...
Receptionist: Have you tried kayaking before?
Emma: No, I haven't.
Receptionist: OK, so you'll need the beginner's course.
Emma: 2 ...
Receptionist: It's £60 for a two-day course. The price includes lessons and lunch on both days.
Emma: Do I need any special equipment?
Receptionist: 3 ... We provide life jackets.
Emma: Cool. Is there anything else I need to know?
Receptionist: 4 ... for after the lesson.
Emma: OK, thanks very much.
Receptionist: No problem.

4 Work in pairs and ask for information about an activity. Follow the steps in the Speaking plan.

Speaking plan

Prepare

- Choose one of the adverts on page 74, or use your own ideas.
- Decide on your roles.
- Make notes for your dialogue.

Speak

- Practise your dialogue.
- Use phrases from the **Useful language** box.
- Act out your dialogue without notes.

Reflect

- How can you improve next time?
- Swap roles and choose a new activity.

Now play *Keep moving!*

FAST FINISHER

What's the most exciting experience you've ever had? Write a few sentences about what you did and how you felt.

I went on holiday to Lanzarote and went scuba diving. I felt scared at first, but when I got in the water, I felt really excited!

LS Language summary: Unit 7 SB p. 133

Tourism in New Zealand

I can compare exciting activities in my country with activities in New Zealand.

NEW ZEALAND: THE HOME OF BUNGY JUMPING

Every year, tourists from all over the world visit New Zealand to take part in extreme sports such as mountain biking, jetboating, heli-skiing and white-water rafting. But the most famous extreme sport in New Zealand is bungy jumping, which attracts hundreds of thousands of visitors a year. How did it all begin?

THE HISTORY OF BUNGY JUMPING

Bungy jumping began on the small island of Vanuatu in the South Pacific. A local legend says that a man and his wife had an argument. The woman ran into the forest and climbed a tree to escape from her angry husband. The husband followed her, so the woman tied a vine* around her ankle and jumped from the top of the tree. The man also jumped, but without a vine. The woman landed safely, but her husband fell to the ground and died. It is now an annual tradition for islanders to build tall towers and dive from the top with just a vine around their ankles.

MODERN BUNGY JUMPING

In the 1980s, a New Zealander called A.J. Hackett made the sport of bungy jumping popular. He worked with scientists at the University of Auckland to create special bungy ropes, and he did his first jump in 1986. He wanted to show the world that bungy jumping was safe, so in 1987 he had an idea. He flew to France and he jumped from the Eiffel Tower in Paris. TV cameras filmed the jump, and suddenly everybody wanted to try it! In 1988, A.J. opened the world's first bungy jumping centre at the Kawarau Bridge in Queenstown. That was the beginning of adventure tourism in New Zealand, and since then millions of people of all ages have experienced the excitement of a bungy jump!

** vine = a long, thin plant that grows down from trees in the rainforest*

1 What do you know about New Zealand? Where is it? What is it famous for?

2 7.12 Read and listen to the travel guide. Who brought the sport of bungy jumping to New Zealand?

3 Read the travel guide again and put the events in the correct order.

a A.J. Hackett jumped for the first time.
b People watched the jump on TV.
c A woman from Vanuatu jumped from a tree.
d A.J. Hackett jumped from the Eiffel Tower.
e Other extreme sports became popular in New Zealand.
f The first bungy jump for tourists began.
g More people started jumping with vines.

4 **Word Power** Find four other extreme sports in the text. Can you think of any more extreme sports?

5 **COMPARE CULTURES** Work in pairs or small groups. What extreme sports or adventure activities can tourists do in your country?

6 New Zealand is not just for adventure tourists! Look at the map and match the activities with the pictures.

a Learn about Māori history and culture.
b Relax on beautiful beaches.
c Explore modern cities.
d See whales and dolphins.
e Go hiking in rainforests.
f Go on a *Lord of the Rings* tour.

7 7.13 Melissa and Josh are tourists in New Zealand. Listen to their podcast. Which of the activities from the map are they doing?

8 7.13 Listen again. Choose the things Melissa and Josh do on the tours.

a go inside a small house
b talk to a scientist
c spend the night in a Māori village
d hear traditional songs
e escape from other people
f swim under a waterfall

9 **GET CREATIVE** Work in groups. Make a video blog or prepare a presentation about an exciting tourist attraction or activity in your country.

Now watch the culture video.

FAST FINISHER

Imagine you are going to visit New Zealand. From what you have learned, what would you like to do, and why?

I'd like to ... because ...

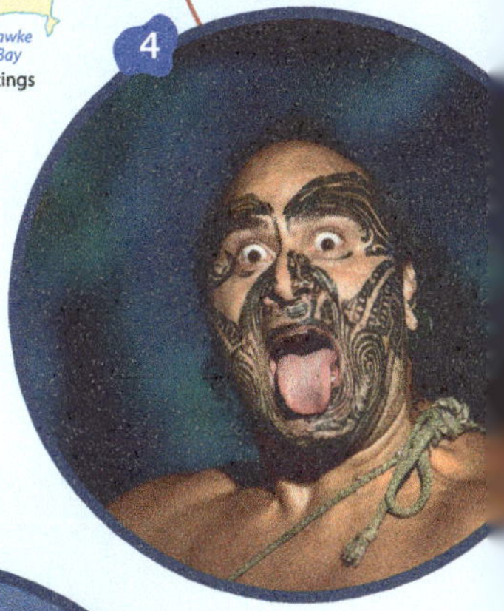

What have you done so far?

WRITING A blog post

I can write a blog post.

1 Work in pairs. Have you been on any school trips? What was your favourite school trip and why?

2 Read Emma's blog about a school trip. Where is Emma? Is she having a good time?

Emma's blog

HOME ABOUT ME LATEST POSTS

Hi, everybody! I'm in Wales on a school trip and I'm having such a good time!

We've done lots of exciting things. We've climbed Mount Snowdon. It was really hard, but the views from the top were amazing! We've also been white-water rafting. It was great fun, but I've never been so scared in my life! I nearly fell out of the boat!

The weather's fantastic – it's so warm. Tomorrow morning, we're going to a beach and we're going to go paddle boarding. Then, in the afternoon, we're going to go on this zip wire. It's the fastest in the world. We're all really excited!

I've bought souvenirs for all my family – a Welsh dragon for Mum, a Welsh football scarf for Dad and a T-shirt for my brother. I can't wait to tell them all about the trip!

3 Read the blog again. Which of the things on the list has Emma done? Write sentences with the present perfect.

SCHOOL TRIP

- go white-water rafting
- go on a zip wire
- go shopping for souvenirs
- go paddle boarding
- climb a mountain

4 Look at the **Useful language**. How do you say these expressions in your language?

Useful language

Describing things you've done

We've done lots of exciting things.
We've climbed ... / been to ... / seen ...
It was amazing / great fun!
Tomorrow, we're going to go to ...

5 Read the **Look!** box. Complete the sentences using *so* or *such a/an*.

Look! *so* and *such*

We use ***so*** and ***such*** to make our opinions stronger.
We use ***so*** + adjective:
*It's **so** warm.*
We use ***such*** + ***a/an*** + adjective + noun phrase:
*I'm having **such a** good time!*

1 We had ... exciting day.
2 The beach was ... beautiful.
3 I bought ... funny souvenir for my best friend!
4 When she got home, she was ... tired.
5 We were ... disappointed with the hotel.
6 It was ... long journey.

6 Imagine you are on a school trip. Write a blog post about it. Follow the steps in the **Writing plan**.

Writing plan

Prepare

› Make notes about your school trip. Where are you? What activities have you done so far? Did you enjoy them?
› What are you doing tomorrow? How are you feeling about it? What souvenirs have you bought?

Write

› Organize your ideas into paragraphs:
  - Introduction.
  - What you've done.
  - What you're going to do next.
› Use the expressions from the **Useful language** box.

Check

› Check your grammar: present perfect, *be going to*.
› Check *so* and *such*.
› Check your spelling.

W Writing summary WB p. 90 E Exams: Unit 7 SB p. 124 L Language summary: Unit 7 SB p. 133

You've got a friend in me 8

Vocabulary: Relationships; Kind acts | **Grammar:** Present perfect with *for* and *since*; Present perfect and past simple | **Speaking:** Persuading | **Writing:** A description of a friend

VOCABULARY Relationships

I can talk about relationships with friends and family.

1 8.1 **Match the verbs in the box with the pictures in the questionnaire. Listen, check and repeat.**

argue (with someone) be kind (to someone) be rude (to someone) get angry (with someone) get on well (with someone) hang out (with someone) look after (someone) make (someone) laugh say sorry (to someone) shout (at someone)

2 Copy and complete the table with the verbs from Exercise 1.

Positive	Negative
be kind	*argue*

3 Complete each question with one word from Exercise 1. Ask and answer the questionnaire in pairs.

FRIENDS AND FAMILY QUESTIONNAIRE

a Do you get ... well with your family?

b Do your parents sometimes get ... with you? Why?

c Do you ever ... with your friends? What about?

d If you're ... to someone, do you always say sorry later?

e Where do you usually hang ... with your friends?

f Which of your friends and family ... you laugh the most?

g Do you sometimes look ... your younger relatives? Who? When?

h If you have upset someone, what's the best way to say ...?

5

6

7

8

4 Write four or five sentences about your partner's answers.

Joanna gets on well with her parents. She often argues with her brother.

Now watch the vlog.

FAST FINISHER

Think about a person you get on well with. Why do you get on well together?

I get on well with my friend Ana. She's very kind. We're both interested in ...

1

2

3

4

9

10

LS Language summary: Unit 8 SB p. 134

A special friend

READING

I can identify correct and incorrect information in a text.

1 8.2 **Work in pairs. Look at the pictures and the title of the article. Discuss the questions. Read and listen to check your ideas.**

1 What are the animals?
2 How and why do you think they became friends?
3 What do you think they do together?

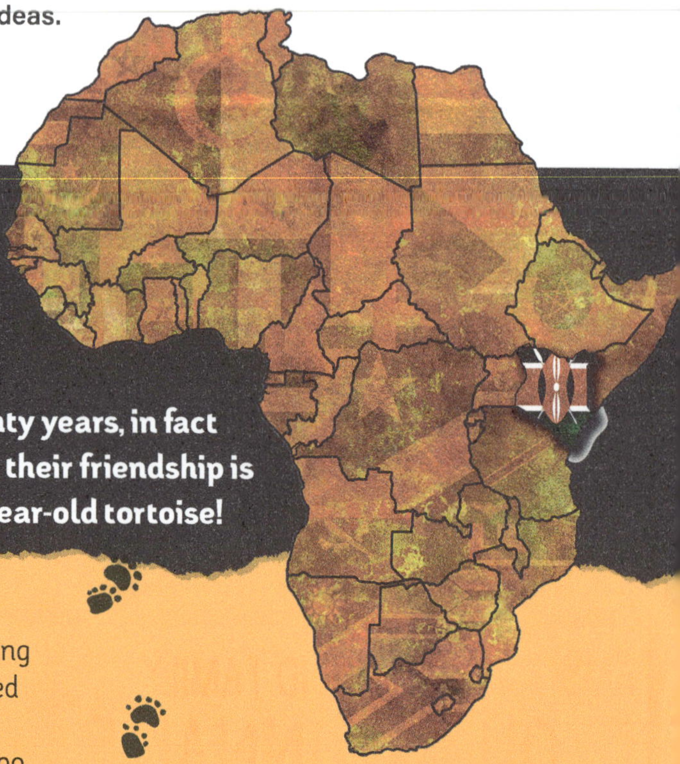

An unusual friendship

Owen and Mzee have been friends for nearly twenty years, in fact since Owen was a baby. But what's unusual about their friendship is that Owen is a hippopotamus and Mzee is a 130-year-old tortoise!

Their story began in Kenya on the east coast of Africa when heavy rain flooded the river where Owen lived. The fast-moving water separated the young hippo from his mother, and carried him all the way to the ocean. Luckily, some fishermen found the hippo, on his own and close to death, and took him to a zoo. Owen has lived there with his new family since that day.

When Owen first arrived at the zoo, there weren't any other hippos, so the zookeepers put him with Mzee, an elderly female giant tortoise. They didn't get on well at first – Mzee preferred being alone – but after a while, they became good friends. They swam and played together, and Mzee looked after Owen like a parent looks after a child. Owen even started behaving like a tortoise! He shared Mzee's food and he slept at night instead of during the day like other hippos.

Owen is now too big to live with Mzee, so the zookeepers have moved him to be with another hippo called Cleo. Owen and Cleo have also become good friends, but Owen hasn't forgotten his old pal, Mzee! Their story is a powerful symbol of friendship, and shows us that if we accept each other's differences, we can all learn to be friends.

2 Read the article again. Are the sentences true (T) or false (F)? Correct the false sentences.

1 Owen became friends with Mzee almost twenty years ago.
2 There was no rain where Owen lived in Africa.
3 Owen was with his mother when the fishermen found him.
4 Owen and Mzee became friends immediately.
5 Mzee was like a mother to Owen.
6 Hippos usually sleep at night.
7 Owen doesn't live with Mzee now.
8 Owen and Cleo don't get on well together.

3 Word Power Find words or phrases in the article that have the same meaning as these words.

1 alone
2 very big
3 old
4 some time later
5 friend
6 sign

4 THINK CRITICALLY Discuss in pairs. What makes a good friendship? Why are friendships important?

5 FIND OUT How long do hippos and giant tortoises usually live?

GRAMMAR Present perfect with *for* and *since*

I can talk about something that started in the past and is still true now.

Now watch the grammar animation.

1 **Read the sentences in the grammar box. Copy and complete the rules with *for* and *since*.**

Owen and Mzee **have been** friends **for** nearly twenty years.
Owen and Mzee **have been** friends **since** Owen was a baby.
It **hasn't rained for** a few months.
It **hasn't rained since** March.

Rules

We use the present perfect + *for* or *since* to talk about something that began in the past and is still true now.

We use [1] ... + a length of time.

We use [2] ... + a point in time.

2 **Copy and complete the table with the words and expressions in the box.**

~~2019~~ seven o'clock five days ~~a long time~~ four hours I was twelve Monday October ten minutes three months two weeks yesterday

for	since
a long time	*2019*

3 **Complete the sentences with *for* or *since*.**

1 She's worn the same socks ... three days.
2 I've been friends with Fernando ... 2018.
3 He's had a girlfriend ... six months.
4 We haven't done any exercise ... weeks.
5 She's worked as a journalist ... she left university.
6 I've been awake ... five o'clock this morning.

4 8.3 **Complete the text. Use the present perfect form of the verb in brackets and *for* or *since*. Listen and check.**

My best friend by Joe, 14

My best friend is called Anna. I*'ve known* (know) her *since* I was eight, and we [1] ... (be) friends [2] ... nearly three years. We're both mad about football. I [3] ... (support) Manchester City [4] ... over ten years, and she [5] ... (be) a fan of Manchester United [6] ... she was little. We always get on really well, but we sometimes argue about which is the best team. Luckily, we [7] ... (not argue) [8] ... a few weeks!

5 **Write true sentences with *for* or *since*, and the ideas below.**

KNOW MY BEST FRIEND
BE AT THIS SCHOOL
LIVE IN MY HOME
HAVE A PHONE
STUDY ENGLISH
BE A FAN OF ...

6 **Work in pairs and compare your answers to Exercise 5. Who has done each thing for the longest time?**

FUN FACT

The world's oldest football club is Sheffield F.C. It has existed since 1857!

FAST FINISHER

Imagine you're a famous person. Write sentences with *for* and *since* about your life.

I've been an actor for ten years. I've lived in a big house in Hollywood since last year.

LS Language summary: Unit 8 SB p. 134

Be kind!

VOCABULARY and LISTENING Kind acts

I can answer *Wh-* questions when I listen.

WORLD KINDNESS DAY

November 13th is World Kindness Day. On this day, people try to make the world a better place by doing kind acts – big and small! What can you do? Here are eight simple ideas:

1 ... your seat to someone on the bus

2 ... someone sitting alone to have lunch with you

3 ... your teacher after a lesson

4 ... from the street

5 ... at everybody you see

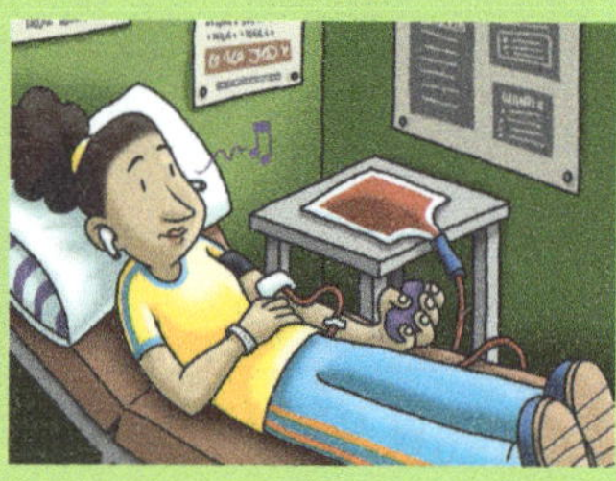

6 ... blood

7 ... for charity

8 ... someone with their shopping bags

1 **Discuss as a class. Have you heard of World Kindness Day? What do you think it is? Give some examples of what people might do on this day.**

2 8.4 **Read about World Kindness Day. Complete the eight kind acts with the verbs and expressions in the box. Listen, check and repeat.**

give help invite offer
pick up litter raise money
smile thank

3 **Work in pairs. Which of the things in Exercise 2 do you do, and how often?**

A: I always offer my seat to elderly people on the bus.

B: Really? I sometimes do that, too.

4 8.5 **Read the tweet. Listen to the interview. Why is Noah doing eighteen kind acts?**

Noah Harris
@NoahHarris795
Follow

It's World Kindness Day today and I'm doing 18 kind acts. Listen to the interview with me here!

3:15 p.m. – 13 Nov – Newcastle

5 20 9

5 8.5 **Listen again and answer the questions.**

1 Where was Noah yesterday morning?
2 Who was he with, and what were they doing?
3 Why does Noah want to change people's ideas about teenagers?
4 What other kind acts has Noah done?
5 When did Noah give blood?
6 How did he feel before and after?

LS Language summary: Unit 8 SB p. 134

GRAMMAR Present perfect and past simple

I can talk about experiences and past actions.

Now watch the grammar animation.

1 **Read the grammar box. Copy and complete the rules with *present perfect* or *past simple*.**

Present perfect	Past simple
I'**ve helped** people with their shopping.	Yesterday morning, we **picked up** rubbish.
I'**ve given** blood.	I **gave** blood on Monday.

Rules

We use the [1] ... to talk about an experience. We use it when we aren't interested in when it happened, only the fact that it happened.

We use the [2] ... to give more details about a finished action in the past. We often mention the exact time when it happened.

2 **Copy and complete the sentences. Use the present perfect or past simple.**

1 Noah ... a lot of people. (help)
2 On Monday, he ... his neighbour's shopping. (carry)
3 Yesterday evening, he ... his grandad's dog for a walk. (take)
4 He ... a lot of interviews on radio. (do)
5 He ... on TV. (not appear)
6 Yesterday, a photo of Noah and his friends ... in the newspaper. (be)

3 **PRONUNCIATION Present perfect and past simple**

8.6 **Listen and repeat.**

1 he helped / he's helped
2 I lived / I've lived
3 they worked / they've worked
4 we tried / we've tried

4 8.7 **Listen and write the sentences you hear.**

5 **Look at each pair of sentences. Decide which needs the present perfect and which needs the past simple. Write the sentences in your notebook.**

1 a I / see / all the James Bond films.
  b I / see / the most recent film / at the weekend.
2 a Layla / break / her arm / last month.
  b Really? I / never break / my arm.
3 a David / travel / to a lot of different places.
  b David / travel / all around China / two years ago.
4 a you / ever / run / a marathon?
  b No, but I / run / a half marathon / last year.

6 **Look at the questionnaire and write the questions in your notebook.**

1 Have you ever raised money for charity?

HAVE YOU EVER ...

1 (raise) money for charity?
2 (offer) your seat to someone on the bus?

3 (cook) dinner for your family or (make) a cake?
4 (see) a thunderstorm?
5 (eat) insects?
6 (write) a story?

7 **Ask and answer the questions from Exercise 6 in pairs. If your partner answers 'yes', ask another question in the past simple to find out more. Use the ideas below.**

A: Have you ever raised money for charity?
B: Yes, I have.
A: When did you do that?
B: Last year. I ran 10 km and I raised 50 euros.

When did you ... ?
Where did you ... ?
What did you ... ?

FAST FINISHER

Write sentences about your classmates' answers to the questionnaire.

Julio has cooked dinner for his family. He made spaghetti last week.

LS Language summary: Unit 8 SB p. 134

KEEP TALKING!

Come on, it'll be fun!

READING and LISTENING

I can understand notices and adverts.

1 **Look at the noticeboard. Have you ever helped with or done any of the things on the board?**

COMMUNITY NOTICEBOARD

a

Beach Clean

When: Saturday, 10 May, 11 a.m. to 4 p.m.
Where: South Beach
We need helpers to pick up plastic and other rubbish from the beach. We'll give you gloves and bags. Afterwards, we'll all go to the beach café for a drink or an ice cream! Interested? Please email us!
beachclean@mail.co.uk

b

WANTED!

Helpers for our after-school club

Have you worked with children? Can you work at least one afternoon a week, from Monday to Friday? Then we need you at our after-school club for five-to-ten-year-olds. You must be happy to organize activities, prepare snacks for the children, and help with homework.
Contact jane@hillviewschool

c

CHARITY BIKE RIDE

Sunday, 11 May, 10 a.m.

Queen's Park

Join our bike ride and help to raise money for charity. Children must be thirteen or older to take part. All cyclists, including adults, must wear a helmet. Cost: £10 per person. All the money we raise will go to the local hospital.

d

CAKE SALE

Bournemouth School
Friday, 16 May, 3.30–4.30 p.m.
We're having a cake sale!
Please bake a cake or make some cookies to help to raise money for new school computers. Bring your cakes to the school office before the day of the sale. The sale will be in the school playground, or in the school hall if the weather is wet.

2 **Read the notices again and choose the correct answers.**

1 If you'd like to help with the beach clean, you should …
   a go to the beach café.
   b take your own gloves.
   c contact the organizers.
2 The notice for the bike ride says that …
   a children under thirteen must be with an adult.
   b only teenagers and adults can do the ride.
   c the bike ride goes from the park to the hospital.
3 After-school club helpers …
   a have to look after the children when school finishes.
   b must be free every day from Monday to Friday.
   c don't need experience with children.
4 For the cake sale, you should …
   a take your cakes to the school on Friday, 16 May.
   b tell the school office if you are planning to go to the sale.
   c go to the school hall to buy a cake if it's raining.

3 8.8 **Listen to three dialogues and match them with three of the notices from the noticeboard.**

4 8.8 **Listen again and answer the questions.**

1 Dialogue 1: Has Will made cakes before? When?
2 Dialogue 2: How many bags has Freddie filled? Where is Lydia's water bottle?
3 Dialogue 3: Has Megan ever worked with children? What has she done?

SPEAKING Persuading

I can persuade someone to do something.

1 8.9 **Listen and read. What does Lauren want to do next Saturday? Does Grant want to do it?**

Lauren: There's a beach clean on Saturday. Do you fancy doing it with me?
Grant: Mmm, I'm not sure. I've got a busy week, so I want to relax on Saturday.
Lauren: Come on, it'll be fun.
Grant: I'll think about it.
Lauren: We really should do it. They need volunteers and it's important. We all use the beach, so we should all help to keep it clean.
Grant: I suppose so.
Lauren: Think of the birds and animals in the sea that it will help. Plastic is so dangerous for wildlife.
Grant: That's true. OK, you've persuaded me! I'll come.
Lauren: Cool! It starts at ten o'clock. Why don't we meet at the bus stop at half past nine?
Grant: Great. See you then.

2 8.10 **Listen and repeat the Useful language.**

Useful language

Persuading	Responding
Do you fancy ... with me?	I'm not sure.
Come on, it'll be fun!	I'll think about it.
We really should do it.	I suppose so.
Think of ...	You've persuaded me!

3 8.11 **Copy and complete the dialogue with the words in the box. Listen and check.**

come coming persuaded suppose sure

Rob: I'm going to the cinema on Saturday afternoon. Do you fancy [1] ... with me?
Ivy: I'm not [2] ... . I've got a lot of homework.
Rob: [3] ... on, it'll be fun!
Ivy: I'll think about it.
Rob: You should come. You can do your homework on Sunday.
Ivy: I [4] ... so.
Rob: Ben and Alice are going to be there, too.
Ivy: OK, you've [5] ... me!
Rob: Great. We're meeting outside the cinema at three o'clock.
Ivy: Cool. See you then.

4 **Work in pairs. Persuade your partner to join you to do something. Follow the steps in the Speaking plan.**

Speaking plan

Prepare

- Choose the cake sale or charity bike ride from page 84, or your own event.
- Decide on your roles. Student A, think of reasons to take part. Student B, think of reasons not to take part.
- Make notes for your dialogue.

Speak

- Practise your dialogue.
- Use phrases from the **Useful language** box.
- Act out your dialogue without notes.

Reflect

- How can you improve next time?
- Swap roles and choose a different event.

Now play *Keep moving!*

FAST FINISHER

Make a list of things you can find or see at the beach.
sand, sea, dolphin ...

LS Language summary: Unit 8 SB p. 134

REAL CULTURE!

The Story of Comic Relief

I can understand information about a charity.

1 Comic Relief is a charity based in the UK. It raises money to help tackle some of the world's biggest problems. Since 1985, Comic Relief has raised over £1 billion to support people living difficult lives in the UK and around the world.

2 In 1985, a group of friends founded Comic Relief. They wanted to use comedy and laughter to raise money and change lives in Africa and the UK. They later invited comedians, actors and pop stars to take part in a special TV show – Red Nose Day.

3 The first Red Nose Day took place in 1988. During the show, viewers at home could donate money to the charity. It was very successful. More than 30 million people watched it and it raised £15 million.

4 Now Comic Relief has a special TV show for Red Nose Day every year. People can wear Red Noses and do fun things to raise money and support the charity. And in 2004, Sport Relief also started, encouraging people to use sport to raise money and change lives.

5 A lot of schools take part in Red Nose Day. For example, students make and sell cakes, or organize 'dressing-up days', when students (and sometimes teachers) pay money to wear pyjamas or funny costumes to school!

6 Celebrities also take part. J.K. Rowling wrote two short books based on her famous Harry Potter series for Comic Relief, and a lot of pop stars have recorded and sold songs for the charity.

7 The money raised by Comic Relief has helped more than 90 million people around the world. The charity tackles homelessness, supports children, fights fear and violence and supports people who have mental health problems.

8 Through comedy, entertainment and sport, the charity has shown that we can all help to make the world a better and fairer place.

1 **Look at the pictures. What do you think the article is about?**

2 8.12 **Read and listen to *The Story of Comic Relief*. Are the sentences true (T) or false (F)?**

1. Comic Relief started more than 30 years ago.
2. The charity raised £1 billion in its first year.
3. The charity helps adults and children.
4. It only helps people in the UK.
5. On Red Nose Day, ordinary people raise money for the charity.
6. Some children and adults wear funny clothes.
7. A lot of famous people have helped to raise money.
8. The Comic Relief TV programme happens every year.

3 **Read the text again and complete the sentences with a number or phrase from the text. Write one, two or three words.**

1. Comic Relief raises money for people in the UK and the rest of … .
2. The charity started in … .
3. The friends organized a special … with comedians, actors and pop stars.
4. Now a lot of people … in Red Nose Day.
5. With the money it raises, Comic Relief wants to make a … world.

4 **Word Power** **Match words 1–6 from the article with definitions a–f.**

1. tackle (verb)
2. comedians (noun)
3. donate (verb)
4. homelessness (noun)
5. fear (noun)
6. violence (noun)

a. to give money to an organization, especially a charity
b. to make the effort to deal with a difficult situation
c. actions which hurt people
d. the feeling you have when something frightening may happen
e. people who make others laugh by telling jokes and funny stories
f. when you have no home

5 **COMPARE CULTURES** **Work in pairs or small groups. Discuss the questions.**

1. What charities in your country do you know? Who, or what, do they help?
2. Do you have TV shows in your country that raise money for charity?

6 **Read the website. Who are the people in the picture? What are they doing and why?**

Home | About | News | **Events**

KILIMANJARO

For this year's Red Nose Day, nine brave celebrities are climbing Africa's highest mountain. They're doing it to raise money for Comic Relief. You can listen to our daily podcast and donate your money here.

LISTEN | DONATE

7 8.13 **Listen to the podcast. How high is Kilimanjaro? Do the celebrities reach the top of the mountain?**

8 8.13 **Listen again and answer the questions.**

1. Name three of the jobs that the celebrities do.
2. For how many hours will the team walk on Day 1?
3. On Day 4, how are the celebrities feeling?
4. On Day 7, what is the weather like at the top of the mountain?
5. How much money have the celebrities raised?

9 **GET CREATIVE** **Work in small groups. Choose a charity, then think of ideas to raise money for the charity. Present your ideas to the class.**

- What is your charity? Who, or what, does your charity help?
- What are you going to do to raise money for your charity?

Now watch the culture video.

FAST FINISHER

Imagine you are climbing a mountain and you have just reached the top. Describe how you feel and what you can see.

Best friends forever!

WRITING A description of a friend

I can write a description of a friend.

1 Read Olivia's description of her best friend. Discuss in pairs. Have you got anything in common with Martha?

My best friend
by Olivia

My best friend is called Martha, and we've known each other for about five years. We met when my family moved house. Martha lives in the same street, and on my first day in the new house, she knocked on the door and introduced herself. We've been friends since that day!

Martha's got long dark hair, beautiful brown eyes, and a big smile! I like her because she's friendly and kind, and she makes me laugh with her jokes. She's really into sport, especially volleyball and basketball, and she's won a lot of competitions. We go to different schools, but we often hang out together after school and at the weekend.

We've got a lot in common, for example, we both like dance music and action films, and most of the time we get on really well. We sometimes argue about little things, but we've never had a big argument. Martha's a really important person to me and I'm sure we'll be friends forever!

2 Look at the **Useful language**. How do you say these expressions in your language?

Useful language

Describing someone you know well

We've known each other for ...
We've been friends since ...
We met when ...
I like him/her because ...
He/She's into ...
We've got a lot in common, for example, ...

3 Read the **Look!** box. Think of more adjectives for columns 1–3.

Look! **Adjective order**

When we use two or more adjectives before a noun, they usually come in this order:

opinion	size/shape	colour	noun
–	*long*	*dark*	*hair*
beautiful	–	*brown*	*eyes*

*Martha's got **long dark** hair.*
*She's got **beautiful brown** eyes.*

4 In your notebook, write the words in the correct order.

1 My cousin Eli is a ... (little / boy / friendly).
2 He's got ... (hair / fair / short).
3 He often wears a pair of ... (cool / trainers / blue).
4 His dad has got a ... (brown / big / beard).
5 His mum has got ... (long / hair / blonde / lovely).

5 Write a description of your best friend. Follow the steps in the **Writing plan.**

Writing plan

Prepare

› Make notes about your friend:
- when and where you met
- his/her appearance and personality
- his/her interests and what you have in common.

Write

› Organize your ideas into paragraphs.
› Use the expressions from the **Useful language** box.

Check

› Check your grammar: present perfect and past simple.
› Check the order of adjectives and your spelling.

Changes

9

Vocabulary: Life stages: nouns and adjectives; School rules | **Grammar:** *used to*; *have to* and *don't have to*; *must* and *mustn't*; Indefinite pronouns | **Speaking:** Talking about rules | **Writing:** An email

VOCABULARY Life stages: nouns and adjectives

I can talk about different life stages.

1 9.1 **Match the words in the box with the pictures. Some words go with more than one picture. Listen, check and repeat.**

Adjectives: elderly grown-up married middle-aged retired

Nouns: adult newborn baby teenager toddler young adult

2 Copy the timeline into your notebook. Add the life stages from Exercise 1.

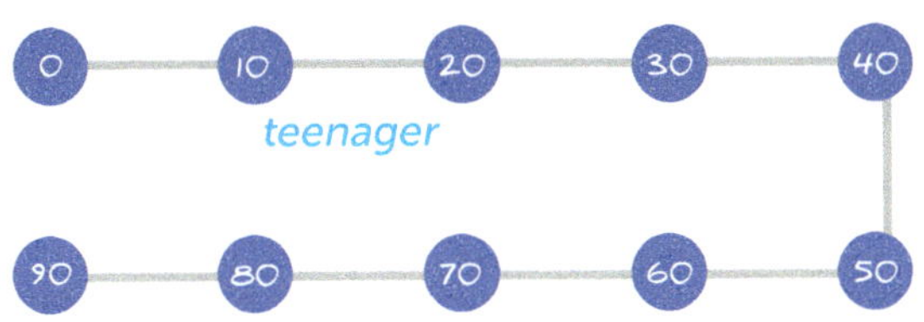

3 When do people usually do these things? Answer in your notebook.

take your driving test
when you're a teenager or young adult

1 learn to walk
2 get grey hair
3 cry at night
4 leave home
5 have children
6 celebrate your 50th birthday
7 start a new hobby, such as golf or walking

4 Read the Look! box. How do we say the following: 30s, 40s, 60s, 70s, 80s? Rewrite sentences 1–5.

Look! Talking about age

To talk about age, we use:
I'm ***in my teens***. (I'm between 13 and 19)
She's ***in her twenties***. (She's between 20 and 29.)
He's ***in his fifties***. (He's between 50 and 59.)

1 My uncle is between 30 and 39.
2 Jack's mum is between 40 and 49.
3 A lot of people retire between 60 and 69.
4 My grandparents are between 70 and 79.
5 I guess she's between 80 and 89.

5 Work in pairs. Ask and answer the questions.

1 What's your earliest memory as a child?
2 What do you think is the best age to be? Why?
3 What's good and bad about being the age you are now?
4 Do you know many elderly people? How are their lives different from your life?

Now watch the vlog.

FAST FINISHER

Write more things that people often do at the life stages in Exercise 1.

Young adult: vote, ...

A life-changing decision

READING

I can identify the main topic of a paragraph.

1 **Read the title of the article. What is a refugee? Complete the definition with the words in the box.**

country	dangers	person	war

refugee

A [1] … who escapes from their [2] … because of [3] … , violence or other [4] … .

FROM TEENAGE REFUGEE TO OLYMPIC SWIMMER

1 …

Before the war in Syria changed her life, Yusra Mardini used to be like any other teenager. She used to see friends, go to school, and listen to music. She and her sister, Sarah, loved swimming, and they used to train regularly. Yusra loved watching sport on TV and she used to dream of becoming an Olympic athlete.

2 …

In 2011, a civil war began in Syria. Yusra often used to see soldiers in the street and hear the sound of gunfire. She continued to swim, but she didn't use to feel safe. Finally, her parents decided they needed to escape from Syria. The plan was for Yusra and Sarah to leave for Germany first, and for the rest of the family to follow later.

3 …

Yusra was just seventeen when she and her sister said goodbye to their parents. They travelled to Turkey, and then by boat to Greece. There they joined thousands of other refugees who were escaping the war, and together they began the long journey on foot, by train and by bus to Germany, where they hoped to build a new life.

4 …

The sisters finally reached Germany and began a new life there. In 2016, after lots of hard work, Yusra achieved her dream and competed in the Olympics for the first ever refugee team. She didn't win a medal, but that wasn't important. Yusra wanted to make other refugees proud, and inspire them to believe in their dreams again. Yusra now lives in Berlin with her family. Her life is very different from how it used to be, but Yusra is happy that it's peaceful.

2 9.2 **Read and listen to the article and answer the questions.**

1 Where did Yusra live before she became a refugee?
2 Why did she leave?
3 Where did she go?
4 How did she get there?
5 Where does she live now? Who with?

3 **Read the article again and match topics a–f to paragraphs 1–4. There are two extra topics.**

a A new life in a new country
b An unusual teenager
c The journey to Europe
d A normal childhood
e A job in Germany
f The start of the violence

4 **Word Power** **Complete the text with the correct form of the blue words from the article.**

If you want to be an Olympic champion, you need to [1] … very hard for many years. Most [2] … will never make it, but a lucky few will [3] … at the Olympic Games as part of their country's [4] … . If you're one of the best, you may win a bronze, silver or gold [5] … , and you may even break a world record.

5 **THINK CRITICALLY** **What challenges do you think Yusra faced in her new life in Germany? What questions would you like to ask her?**

6 **FIND OUT** **How many refugees are there in the world? What are some of the countries they come from? What are some of the reasons they leave their countries?**

GRAMMAR *used to*

I can talk about actions that happened regularly in the past.

Now watch the grammar animation.

1 Read the grammar box. Copy and complete the rules with the words in the box.

aren't happened negative were

Affirmative

She **used to** see soldiers on the street.
Yusra and Sarah **used to** train regularly.

Negative

Her home city **didn't use to** be dangerous.
People **didn't use to** feel scared.

Questions	Short answers
Did she **use to** see her friends after school?	Yes, she **did**. / No, she **didn't**.
Did you **use to** live in a big house?	Yes, I **did**. / No, I **didn't**.

Rules

We use *used to* to talk about:

- actions that [1] ... regularly in the past.
- things that [2] ... true in the past, but [3] ... true now.

The [4] ... form of *used to* is *didn't use to* (not *didn't used to*).

2 Copy and complete the sentences. Use the correct form of *used to* and the verb in brackets.

Yusra *used to live* (live) in Damascus, the Syrian capital.

1 It ... (not / be) dangerous to live in Damascus.
2 Tourists ... (visit) the city's beautiful buildings and colourful markets.
3 Yusra and her sister ... (swim) three times a week.
4 They ... (train) with their father.
5 **A:** ... he ... (be) a swimmer, too?
B: Yes, he ... .
6 There ... (not / be) a war.
7 The family ... (not / see) soldiers on the street.
8 **A:** ... they ... (feel) afraid?
B: No, they ... .

3 Look at the pictures of Ed now and when he was at primary school. Write sentences with the correct form of *used to*.

Ed at primary school, London

Ed now, Manchester

have short hair
Ed used to have short hair.

1 play the violin
2 play the guitar
3 wear glasses
4 like dinosaurs
5 live in Manchester
6 go to school in London

4 Write questions about when you were at primary school. Ask and answer with a partner.

wear a school uniform
A: Did you use to wear a school uniform?
B: Yes, I did. I used to wear grey shorts and a red polo shirt.

1 have a lot of homework
2 your parents / take you to school
3 play games at break time
4 your teacher / read you stories
5 go to any after-school clubs

FUN FACT

The physicist Albert Einstein, the actress Mila Kunis and the singer Rita Ora all used to be refugees before they found a new home in a new country.

FAST FINISHER

Write sentences with *used to* about your family and friends.

My friend Cassie used to have a pet hamster.

LS Language summary: Unit 9 SB p. 135

Different countries, different rules

VOCABULARY and LISTENING School rules

I can listen for the answers to a quiz.

1 9.3 **Match verbs 1–12 with words a–l to make expressions. Listen, check and repeat.**

1 g arrive on time

1	~~arrive~~	a	your classroom tidy
2	chew	b	smartly
3	dress	c	litter
4	drop	d	jewellery
5	follow	e	attention
6	forget	f	bad language
7	keep	g	~~on time~~
8	pay	h	your books
9	put	i	in the corridors
10	run	j	gum
11	use	k	instructions
12	wear	l	your hand up

2 Work in pairs. Copy and complete the school rules with the expressions in Exercise 1. Think about what's normal at most schools.

Do this ✓	Don't do this ✗
arrive on time	*chew gum*

3 Look at the pictures in the quiz. How many school rules in Exercise 2 can you match with them?

4 9.4 **Work in pairs and do the quiz. Are the sentences true (T) or false (F)? Listen and check.**

5 9.4 **Listen again and answer the questions.**

1 Name four other parts of the school that Japanese students help to clean.
2 When do some American students sing the national anthem?
3 Why can't you chew gum in Singapore?
4 Which day don't some French schoolchildren have to go to school?
5 Apart from at school, when do Thai children take off their shoes?
6 Why do teachers in China think it's good for students to have a sleep after lunch?

a

SCHOOLS AROUND THE WORLD

Could you live in another country? Do you know the customs and rules? Try our quiz to find out.

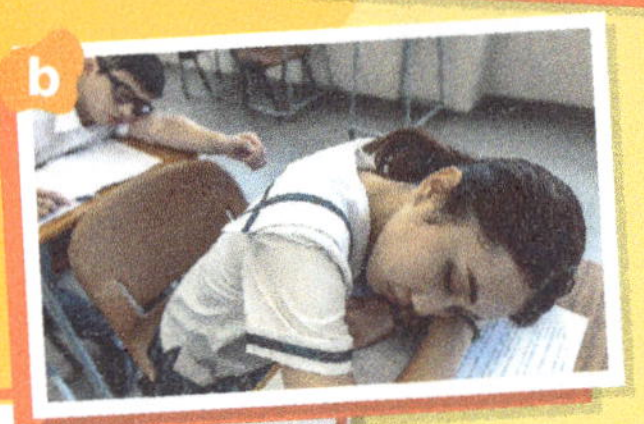
b

c

TRUE or FALSE?

1 In Japan, schoolchildren must clean their classrooms for fifteen to twenty minutes every day.
2 Students in the USA have to sing the national anthem every morning.
3 In Singapore, students and teachers are allowed to chew gum in class.
4 In France, a lot of primary school children only go to school for four days a week.
5 In Peru, if students want to ask a question, they must put both hands up.
6 In Thailand, children have to take off their shoes before they go into class.
7 In some Scottish schools, students who drop litter must pay a fine of £80.
8 In a lot of Chinese schools, children can have a 30-minute sleep on their desks after lunch.

d

f

e

LS Language summary: Unit 9 SB p. 135

GRAMMAR *have to* and *don't have to*; *must* and *mustn't*

I can talk about obligation and rules.

Now watch the grammar animation.

1 **Read the grammar box. Copy and complete the rules with the words in the box.**

different   necessary   not necessary   similar

Affirmative

She **has to** take her shoes off in class.
Children **have to** clean their classrooms.
Students in Japan **must** keep their school clean.

Negative

He **doesn't have to** go to school on Wednesday.
Students **don't have to** sing the national anthem.
In Singapore, you **mustn't** chew gum.

Questions	Short answers
Do you **have to** do any homework tonight?	Yes, I **do**. / No, I **don't**.
Does she **have to** go to school on Wednesday?	Yes, she **does**. / No, she **doesn't**.

Rules

We use *have to* to say that something is [1] … .

We use *don't have to* to say that something is [2] … (but you can do it if you want to).

Have to has a [3] … meaning to *must*.

Don't have to and *mustn't* have completely [4] … meanings.

2 9.5 **Complete the text with the words in the box. Listen and check.**

doesn't have to   don't have to   has to (x2)
have to (x2)   mustn't (x3)

A YEAR IN THE USA

Fifteen-year-old Archie from Sheffield, in the UK, is spending a year in the USA. What's his new school like?

'In Sheffield, we don't start school until 8.45. Here, school starts at 7.30, so I [1] … get up really early!' says Archie. He [2] … leave the house at 6.55 to get the bus and he [3] … be late. 'Students who are late [4] … sit in a separate room for the rest of the lesson,' says Archie.

His school in Sheffield has a uniform. In his new school, Archie [5] … wear a uniform, but he [6] … wear sensible clothes. 'We [7] … wear jeans with holes in them, for example, and girls [8] … wear short skirts.'

What's the best thing about his new school? 'There are a lot of after-school clubs. You [9] … join, but it's a good way to make friends and have fun.'

3 **PRONUNCIATION** ***must* and *mustn't***

9.6 **Listen and repeat. Which letter don't we pronounce in *mustn't*?**

You must be on time.   You mustn't be late.

4 9.7 **Listen and write the sentences you hear.**

5 **Work in pairs and make sentences. What do you have to do at school and at home?**

At school	At home
We have to …	I have to …
We mustn't …	I don't have to …

Indefinite pronouns

I can use indefinite pronouns to refer to people, places and things.

6 **Read the examples. Copy and complete the grammar box with the words in bold.**

Indefinite pronouns

It's traditional to take off your shoes when you visit **someone's** home.
You aren't allowed to chew gum **anywhere**.
Students don't have to do **anything**.

	people	places	things
Affirmative	[1] … / somebody	somewhere	something
Negative / Questions	anyone / anybody	[2] …	[3] …

7 **Complete the sentences with an indefinite pronoun.**

1 I was two minutes late for class, but luckily my teacher didn't say … .
2 I know … who goes to school in France.
3 Did you go … at the weekend?
4 I'm really hungry. I need … to eat.
5 Let's go … quiet where we can talk.
6 Has … seen my phone? I can't find it.

FAST FINISHER

Think of places in your town. Write things you *have to*, *mustn't* and *don't have to* do there.

You don't have to pay to go to the museum.

LS **Language summary: Unit 9** **SB** p. 135

KEEP TALKING!

A school exchange

READING and LISTENING

I can understand a letter about a school exchange.

1 **Discuss as a class. Does your school organize trips out of school? What about exchange trips with schools in other countries?**

OAK PARK SCHOOL

Oak Park School
Park Road
Dublin
Ireland
Telephone: 353 20 917 9935
Email: office@oakpark.dublin.ie

Exchange trip to Valencia, Spain

26th April – 3rd May (in Valencia) and 22nd – 29th June (in Dublin)

Dear Parents

We are pleased to offer your son/daughter the chance to take part in an exchange with a school [1] ... Valencia. This is a great opportunity for students to learn about life in Spain, improve their Spanish, and make [2] ... Spanish friends.

The exchange is open to students aged fifteen and above who [3] ... studying Spanish. They will stay with a Spanish family. The Spanish students [4] ... then stay in your home during their visit to Dublin. Students [5] ... follow the family's rules during their stay.

In Valencia, we will spend one day at school. On the other days, [6] ... will be trips to visit the region. The cost of the exchange includes all flights, trips [7] ... meals. Students will need a small amount of money to spend, and they must have [8] ... passport.

We have run the trip [9] ... ten years, and it is always very popular. If you would [10] ... to reserve a place for your son/daughter, please contact the school office.

Yours sincerely

Ms Silvia Young

Head of Spanish

2 **Look at the letter about a school exchange and answer the questions.**

1 Who is the letter to?
2 Who is the letter from?
3 Which two countries and cities is the exchange between?
4 When is the exchange?
5 How old do you have to be to go on the exchange?

3 **Read the letter again. In your notebook, write one word for each gap.**

4 9.8 **Listen and check your answers.**

5 9.9 **Listen to the dialogue. When did Sara arrive in Spain? Where is she now?**

6 9.9 **Listen again and answer the questions.**

1 What is Sara's host family like?
2 Why is Sara tired?
3 What is her exchange student's name?
4 What are the house rules?
5 What are they going to do tomorrow?

7 **GET CREATIVE** **Work in small groups. Plan a five-day programme of trips for students from the UK who are visiting your town. Present your ideas to the class.**

SPEAKING Talking about rules

I can talk about rules.

1 9.10 **Fran, from Spain, is in Dublin on the school exchange. Listen and read. What are some of the things he must and mustn't do in Adam's home?**

Adam: Welcome to our home, Fran.
Fran: Thank you. It's a really nice house.
Adam: There are a few rules that I must tell you about. Firstly, you have to take your shoes off when you come in the house, and you aren't allowed to eat food in your bedroom.
Fran: No problem. Is it OK to play music?
Adam: Yes, that's fine, but Mum and Dad go to bed quite early, so we mustn't make a noise after 9 p.m.
Fran: No worries.
Adam: We usually have dinner at about 6.30. You don't have to help with the cooking – Mum and Dad do that – but we all have to help tidy up afterwards.
Fran: It's the same at my house. My sister and I have to lay the table and load the dishwasher.
Adam: Cool. Anyway, those are all the rules. Let's go and have some fun. Do you fancy a game of football at the park?
Fran: Great idea!

2 9.11 **Listen and repeat the Useful language.**

Useful language

Talking about rules

You have to ...
You aren't allowed to ...
Is it OK to ...?
You mustn't ...
You don't have to ...
We all have to ...

3 9.12 **Copy and complete the dialogue with the words in the box. Listen and check.**

aren't allowed | don't have to | Is it OK | must (x2) | mustn't

Coach: Welcome to the judo club. There are some rules I must tell you about. Firstly, you [1] ... to wear shoes on the judo mat, and you [2] ... wear any jewellery. Girls [3] ... wear a white T-shirt under their judo top, but boys [4] ... wear one if they don't want to. Yes?
Pupil: [5] ... to have long hair?
Coach: Yes, but you [6] ... tie it back behind your head. Is that clear?
Class: Yes!

4 **Work in pairs. Welcome an exchange student to your school and explain some of the rules. Follow the steps in the Speaking plan.**

Speaking plan

Prepare

› Make notes about your school rules:
- things you have to do
- things you aren't allowed to / mustn't do
- things it's OK to do

Speak

› Welcome the student to your school and start the dialogue.
› Use phrases from the **Useful language** box.
› Practise your dialogue. Then act it out without notes.

Reflect

› How can you improve next time?
› Swap roles and choose a new activity.

Now play *Keep moving!*

FAST FINISHER

Imagine you are the manager of a sports centre. Write some rules for using the gym, the swimming pool, etc.

LS Language summary: Unit 9 SB p. 135

Multicultural USA

I can compare a community in the USA to a community in my country.

LATINO AMERICANS IN THE USA

The United States is the most multicultural nation in the world. Many Americans belong to two cultures: the country they call home, and the country their parents or grandparents came from. One of the most important groups are Latino Americans, whose culture has had an important influence on the USA. How? Let's take a look.

There are about 59 million Latino Americans in the USA – Americans whose families originally come from South and Central America, Mexico and parts of the Caribbean. That's 18% of the population!

Spanish speakers have been in North America for longer than English speakers, and their influence is everywhere – from the names of American cities, such as Los Angeles and San Francisco, to music, to food.

FOOD

Americans love to visit Latin American restaurants, particularly Mexican, Cuban and Peruvian, or cook Latino food at home. Mexican dishes such as *tacos* and *burritos* are part of American life. *Ceviche* – raw fish with lime juice – comes from Peru and is another popular dish.

LANGUAGE

Spanish is the second most spoken language in the United States. Many Latino families speak Spanish at home, so a lot of Latino Americans are bilingual. There are even Spanish-language and bilingual TV and radio stations.

MUSIC

Latino music is very popular in the USA – from traditional salsa dance music and reggaeton, to Tex-Mex (a type of Mexican folk music) and Latino pop. Best-selling Latino musicians include Selena Gomez, Camila Cabello, Pitbull and Bruno Mars.

CELEBRATIONS

There are lots of festivals that celebrate Latino culture in the USA. One of the biggest festivals is *Cinco de Mayo*, which happens every year on or around 5 May with parades, parties and traditional Mexican *mariachi* music.

1 **Look at the title of the article. How many countries in Latin America can you name?**

2 9.13 **Read and listen to the article and answer the questions.**

1 After English, what is the most spoken language in the USA?
2 What are some of the ways speakers of this language have influenced the USA?

3 **Read the article again. Match 1–6 to a–e, then complete the sentences with the verbs in the box.**

1 d 59 million Latino Americans live in the USA.

come ~~live~~ love sing speak take place

1 ~~59 million Latino Americans ...~~
2 Americans ...
3 *Tacos and burritos* ...
4 A lot of Latino Americans ...
5 Camila Cabello and Bruno Mars ...
6 *Cinco de Mayo* parades ...

a in May.
b from Mexico.
c Latino pop.
d ~~in the USA.~~
e English and Spanish.
f Latino food.

4 **Word Power** **Look at the list of some of the most spoken languages in the USA. Complete the languages with the correct ending.**

Most spoken languages in the USA

1 Engl
2 Span
3 Chin
4 Fren
5 Vietnam
6 Kore
7 Germ
8 Arab
9 Russ
10 Ital

- an - ch
- ese - ish
- ian - ic

5 **COMPARE CULTURES** **Are there bilingual communities in your country? What languages do they speak? Are there TV and radio stations in other languages?**

6 **You are going to listen to an interview with Dang, who moved to the USA from Vietnam. Before you listen, put the words of the interviewer's questions in the correct order.**

INTERVIEW QUESTIONS

1 did / When / you / to the USA / move / ?
2 was / when you arrived / the hardest thing / What / ?
3 How / from Vietnam / different / school / in the USA / is / ?
4 miss / about Vietnam / What / you / do / ?
5 you / do / What / about the USA / like most / ?

7 9.14 **Listen and check your answers to Exercise 6.**

8 9.14 **Listen again. Make notes about Dang's answers to each question.**

Now watch the culture video.

FAST FINISHER

Think of more questions to ask Dang about his experience in the USA.

What do I need to bring?

WRITING An email

I can write an email to someone who is coming to my country.

1 **Read the email from Azra in Italy. Who is Erin? Why is Azra writing?**

Hi Erin

I'm looking forward to meeting you next month on the school exchange to Bristol. What's the weather like there? What do I need to bring? Is there anything else I need to know?

Bye for now

Azra

2 **Read Erin's reply. Does she answer Azra's questions?**

Hi Azra

I'm looking forward to meeting you, too. It's going to be fun!

Unfortunately, it usually rains a lot in November, so you should bring a raincoat. I suggest that you pack a hat and some gloves, too, as it can be cold. Hopefully, you won't need them.

Do you want to play basketball when you're here? I play every Wednesday at my local sports centre, so if you want to play, bring your sports kit. I have to wear a uniform to school, but luckily, exchange students don't have to! It's a good idea to bring some money, but you won't need much. You don't have to pay for any meals or trips, so it's just for shopping or snacks.

The only other thing to tell you is that we've got a dog, Bella. I sometimes have to take her for a walk after school. I hope you like dogs – she's very cute!

See you soon

Erin

3 **Look at the Useful language. How do you say these expressions in your language?**

Useful language

Giving information

You should ...

I suggest that you ...

You won't need ...

You have to / don't have to ...

4 **Study the Look! box. Find one more adverb in Erin's email for introducing a sentence.**

Look! Opinion adverbs

We sometimes use adverbs to give an opinion at the start of a sentence.

***Unfortunately**, it usually rains a lot in November.*

***Luckily**, exchange students don't have to wear a uniform!*

5 **Rewrite the sentences. Use an opinion adverb.**

It's unfortunate that we have to get up early.

Unfortunately, we have to get up early.

1 It's lucky that I live near a bus stop.
2 I hope that the bus won't be late.
3 It's unfortunate that I've got a lot to do tonight.
4 I hope that the weather will be nice tomorrow.
5 It's lucky that he passed the exam.

6 **Write your own reply to Azra's email in Exercise 1. Follow the steps in the Writing plan.**

Writing plan

Prepare

› Imagine Azra is visiting your school. Make notes about the three questions she asks.

Write

› Organize your answers to Azra's questions in three paragraphs.
› Use the expressions from the **Useful language** box.
› Start and finish your email in a friendly way:
  - *Dear ... / Hi ...*
  - *Bye for now / See you soon / Best wishes*

Check

› Check your grammar: *have to* and *don't have to*.
› Check opinion adverbs and your spelling.

W Writing summary WB p. 92
R Review: Units 7-9 SB pp. 104–105
P Project: Units 7-9 SB pp. 110–111
L Literature: Units 7-9 SB pp. 116–117
E Exams: Unit 9 SB p. 126
LS Language summary: Unit 9 SB p. 135

CONTENTS

REVIEW UNITS 1–3

READING

1 Read about Jen. Complete the text with the words in the box.

along couldn't doesn't every floor hard onto rubbish there was was washing up were chatting while working

How I got my job

Jen Evans is a lifeguard. She tells us how she got her job.

When I left school, my first job was as a kitchen assistant in a restaurant. I did the [1] ..., took out the [2] ... and at the end of the evening, I washed the kitchen [3] ..., ready for the next day. I didn't really like the job, but I couldn't think what else to do.

One day I [4] ... at the beach with some friends. We [5] ... when I heard a shout. There was a boy in the water and he [6] ... swim. I'm a good swimmer, so I quickly ran [7] ... the beach and dived into the sea. I pulled the boy [8] ... the sand and luckily he was OK.

[9] ... a lifeguard on the next beach. He heard what happened and arrived [10] ... I was saving the boy. I talked to him about his job and that's when I decided I wanted to be a lifeguard. I trained [11] ... and now I'm [12] ... on a beach in Cornwall, south-west England.

I love being a lifeguard. It [13] ... feel like a job. I get up early and watch the sunrise [14] ... morning. The beach is my office!

2 Complete the sentences with one word.

1 Jen ... enjoy her first job.
2 She was ... to her friends when she heard the boy in the water.
3 Luckily, Jen could swim ... .
4 Jen ... work in the restaurant now.
5 She ... watches the sunrise in the morning.

LISTENING

3 R1 Look at the film posters, then listen. What type of film is shown in each poster? Choose from the options below. There are three extra options.

action film animated film comedy documentary horror film romantic film science-fiction film

a

b

c

d

4 R1 Listen again. Are the sentences true (T) or false (F)? Correct the false sentences. Listen and check.

1 Max says that *Rise of the Robots* was funny.
2 Kate likes animated films.
3 Max says that *Our Last Summer* was romantic.
4 Max watched *The Rescue* two nights ago.
5 The men in *The Rescue* were both lawyers.
6 Max's brother saw *Paris in Spring* last week.

5 R1 Answer the questions. Write full sentences. Then listen and check.

1 What was the weather like at the weekend?
2 When did Max watch *Rise of the Robots*?
3 Who did he watch it with?
4 Where do the characters in *Our Last Summer* go camping?
5 When did the story of *The Rescue* happen?
6 What was Nick doing when he fell?
7 Why couldn't his friend move?

SPEAKING

6 Work in pairs. Ask and answer questions about the things below.

A: What time do you wake up on a school day?
B: I usually wake up at half past seven.

THINGS IN THE PRESENT

1 What time (you / wake up) on a school day?
2 How (you / usually / get) to school?
3 What (you / wear) today?

THINGS THAT HAPPENED IN THE PAST

4 What (you / have) for dinner last night?
5 Which jobs around the home (you / do) last weekend?
6 What (can / you / do) when you were three?

ACTIONS IN PROGRESS IN THE PAST

7 What (you / do) at eight o'clock this morning?
8 What (you / do) when (this lesson / start)?
9 (it / rain) at this time yesterday?

THE WAY WE DO THINGS (ADVERBS)

10 What things do you usually do (slow)?
11 Do you usually do your homework (careful)?
12 Name something that you do (good), and something that you do (bad).

WRITING

7 Imagine you have one of the jobs in the box, or choose a different job. Write about your job. Use the questions below and the text in Exercise 1 to help you.

farmer journalist mechanic
nurse police officer shop assistant

- What is your name and your job?
- What were you doing before you became a ...?
- Why did you want to be a ...?
- What is a typical day for you?
- What did you do yesterday?
- What do you like about your job?

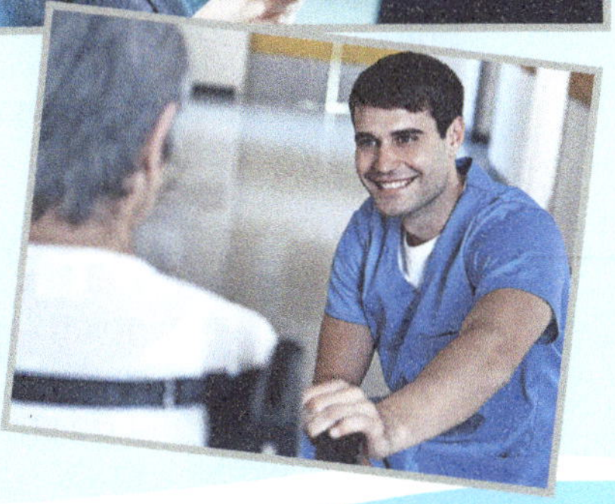

TEST YOUR MEMORY!

- Describe one thing you do every day and one thing you're doing now.
- Name five types of film.
- Choose an age, and say three things that you *could* or *couldn't* do.
- Make three sentences using these adverbs: *easily, well, quietly*.
- Say as many jobs as you can in 30 seconds.
- Describe what was happening when you woke up this morning.
- Name five adjectives to describe a book or a film.
- Say five things you did last weekend.
- Describe the jobs that you and your family do around the home.
- Name five verbs of movement.
- Say what *there was* or *wasn't* in your fridge this morning.
- Name five adverbs or expressions of frequency.

REVIEW UNITS 4–6

READING

1 Choose the correct answers to complete the text.

The fight against plastic

Plastic pollution is one of the [1] *bigger / biggest* problems for our planet. There is [2] *a lot / a lot of* plastic in the oceans, and it gets into the [3] *stomachs / shoulders* of seabirds and other animals. We don't know exactly [4] *how many / how much* animals die from plastic pollution, but scientists think more than one million every year.

We talked to the Adams family, who want to use less plastic.

'Plastic bags are one of [5] *worst / the worst* causes of pollution', says Paul Adams. 'When we go shopping, [6] *we're going / we will* to take a reuseable bag with us from now on. It's only a small thing, but if we [7] *won't / don't* do anything, the problem will only get [8] *worse / worst*.'

'I'm not going to buy bottled water any more,' says his wife, Jane. '[9] *I will / I'm going to* drink only tap water. It's a great way to [10] *save / earn* money, too! Also, I'm only going to buy things like honey and coffee in glass [11] *tins / jars*, not plastic containers.'

Plastic is everywhere, so it [12] *won't / will* be easy to stop using it completely. However, everybody should [13] *try / to try* to make a change.

2 Complete the text with the correct form of the word in brackets. Use *going to*, *will*, comparatives or superlatives.

Jane says: 'Experts predict that plastic pollution [1] ... (double) in the next ten years. That's scary, but if we all try much [2] ... (hard) to use less plastic, we [3] ... (help) to create less waste. We [4] ... (make) fruit juice at home instead of buying it at the supermarket. It's [5] ... (good) for the planet and it's [6] ... (healthy), too. We want to help the environment in other ways, as well. This year, we [7] ... (stay) in the UK for our summer holiday. We love going abroad, but flying is one of the [8] ... (bad) things for the planet.'

LISTENING

3 R2 Listen to the podcast about a summer job. Which topics do Danny and Steve talk about?

food and drink health and medicine money party plans social media

4 R2 Listen again and complete the notes.

My summer job

Name: *Danny Price*
Studying: [1] *... at the University of Manchester*
Summer job: [2] *... helper at a music festival*
Future job: [3] *...*
How much does he earn?: [4] *... a day*
Common health problems at the festival:
[5] ...
[6] ...
[7] ...
Where is he staying?: *In a* [8] ...

5 R2 Complete the sentences with one or two words. Then listen again and check.

1. If he ... enough money, he'll buy a car.
2. People get sunburn because they don't use ... .
3. At a festival, you ... try to eat and drink normally.
4. Yesterday, there was a man with a ... .
5. A girl cut ... on some glass.
6. Danny brought his own ... to sleep in.
7. Steve has got sunburn on his ... .
8. Steve ... go in the sun without a T-shirt and a sun hat.

SPEAKING

6 **Work in pairs. Read the situations and continue the conversations. After each conversation, swap roles and repeat.**

At the doctor's

A: How can I help you?
B: I've got a cold. What should I do?

Borrowing some money from your mum or dad

A: Can you lend me some money?
B: That depends. Why do you need it?

Planning a party

A: I'm going to have a big party for my birthday next month.
B: What are you going to do for it?

WRITING

7 **You are planning a camping trip with your family and friends. Write a paragraph about your plans.**

- When and where are you going to go?
- What are you going to do there?
- What do you think the weather will be like?
- What are you going to take with you?
- What will you do if it rains? What will you do if it's sunny?
- What should and shouldn't you do on your trip?

TEST YOUR MEMORY!

- Make three predictions about how life may be different in the future.
- Say as many parts of the body as you can in 30 seconds.
- Give three pieces of advice to someone who wants to improve their English.
- Say three things that you are doing this evening.
- Make two questions with *How much …?* and two with *How many …?*
- Name five things to do if you're planning a party.
- Say what you'll do if you feel ill tomorrow.
- Name as many food containers as you can in 30 seconds.
- Give the comparative and superlative forms of these adjectives: *easy, exciting, good, bad, far.*
- Name five things to take on a camping trip.
- Say five things that you plan to do in the summer.
- Give the reflexive pronouns for *I, you, he, she, it, we, you, they.*

REVIEW UNITS 7–9

READING

1 Read the text and choose the correct option: A, B or C.

Please don't be worried, but …

Have you [1] … been on an adventure or travelled somewhere exciting? A lot of British [2] … take a 'gap year' – a one-year holiday between secondary school and university – to [3] … new friends and see the world. For their parents, it can be a stressful time! Imagine you're a parent and you get one of these messages from your son or daughter …

Hi, Mum and Dad, I'm having a great time. I [4] … bungy jumping and sky diving. Last week, I [5] … rock climbing. Please don't be [6] …, but while we were climbing, we saw an enormous snake.

I met an English girl on the train, and we [7] … on really well. We're going to rent motorbikes and explore the mountains. I've [8] … ridden a motorbike before and the roads are really narrow! You [9] … ride without a helmet!

We've been here in Mexico [10] … about a week. Most days, we hang [11] … with friends at the beach. Yesterday, we went swimming with sharks! We weren't scared – they were leopard sharks so they aren't dangerous. You [12] … to try it – it's amazing!

	a	b	c
1	a never	b ever	c not
2	a teenagers	b toddlers	c adults
3	a take	b do	c make
4	a 've tried	b tried	c try
5	a went	b 've gone	c go
6	a embarrassed	b worried	c disappointed
7	a took	b got	c put
8	a ever	b never	c badly
9	a mustn't	b don't have to	c should
10	a since	b during	c for
11	a out	b in	c off
12	a should	b must	c have

LISTENING

2 R3 Listen to an interview. What is it about? Choose the correct summary.

a It's about a school where students don't like the new rules.
b It's about a school that is very different from how it used to be.
c It's about a teacher who is celebrating a new job.

3 R3 Complete the sentences and questions from the interview with the words in the box. Listen and check.

become	cheerful	got	have
mustn't	pay	use	worked

1 The students have … really hard.
2 What did it … to be like?
3 When I … a job here five years ago, things were very different.
4 They didn't use to … attention in class.
5 What … you done to change things?
6 They … forget their books, pens or pencils.
7 The students are more … now because we don't have the problems we used to have.
8 They've … happier, kinder and more confident.

4 R3 Complete the answers to the questions. Listen and check.

1 Why is the school celebrating?
Because the students have … .
2 How does the head teacher feel about the changes.
She feels … , but not … .
3 What did students use to do? Give two examples.
Students used to … and they … .
4 What new school rules are there? Give two examples.
Students have to … and they … .
5 What kind of place is the school now?
It's a … and … place to be now.

SPEAKING

5 Work in pairs. Follow the instructions.

1 Ask and answer about experiences in your life. Use the topics in the box and *ever / never*.

- countries • extreme sport • films • food

Have you ever been to Italy?

2 Ask and answer about rules. Use the places in the box and your own ideas. Use *(don't) have to, must / mustn't*.

- at home • at your school • in public places
- in your town • on a plane

What do you have to do at home?

3 Ask and answer about when you were younger. Use the ideas in the box and *used to / didn't use to*.

- daily routine • free time activities • hair style
- toys • TV

When you were six, what time did you use to go to bed?

4 Ask and answer about friends and people in your family. Use the ideas in the box. Use the present perfect with *for / since*, or *ever / never*.

- argue • get on well • hang out
- look after • make you laugh

How long have you known your best friend?
Have you ever argued with him/her?

WRITING

6 **Imagine you and your friends are at an exciting holiday camp, like the one in the advert. Write a paragraph about it. Include all the information below.**

- Say how long you have been there.
- Describe your experiences. What have you done so far?
- Talk about your friends. Are you all getting on well together?
- Say what you did yesterday. How did you feel?
- Describe the rules of the camp.

TEST YOUR MEMORY!

- Describe two things you have to do at home, and two things you don't have to do.
- Give the past participle of these verbs: *ask, eat, meet, see, win*.
- Make three questions with *Have you ever … ?*
- Say three interesting things you've done in your life. Then say when you did them.
- List five adventures on your bucket list.
- Name five adjectives to describe feelings.
- Describe four things you used to do or didn't use to do when you were younger.
- Give two expressions with each of the following verbs: *get, go, make, take*.
- Say three kind acts you have done in the last month.
- Think of three activities you do and say how long you have done them. Use the present perfect with *for* or *since*.
- Name five rules at your school.
- Say four adjectives or nouns to describe people of different ages.

PROJECT UNITS 1–3

TASK

Create a vlog about one week in your life

I can work in pairs and produce a vlog.

PREPARE

a

b

c

d

Monday	I went to the cinema with Ben.
Tuesday	I tidied my room and did the laundry.
Wednesday	I washed the floor.
Thursday	I made dinner for my family.
Friday	I went shopping after school.
Saturday	I did some babysitting.
Sunday	I tried a climbing wall with Markus.

e

f

g

Step 1 **Get ideas**

- Look at the photos. Did you do any of these activities last week?
- Work in pairs. Talk about things you did …
  - in the week / at the weekend
  - together / with your family / with other friends
  - at school / at home / in other places

Step 2 **Choose your activities**

- Work in pairs. Copy the diary above. On each day, write two things you talked about in Step 1.
- Ask each other questions to get more information about the things you did. Use the **Useful language** box to help you. Make notes of the answers.
- Which things are the most interesting to talk about in your vlog? Choose one idea for each day.

Look! **Negotiation**

If you don't agree with your partner about which thing is the most interesting, try to explain your reasons. Listen carefully to each other. Choose ideas from both of you.

Step 3 **Do your research**

- Watch some vlogs. What makes them good or bad? Write down ways to make yours interesting.
- Think about things you can use to make a vlog – a recording device, pens and paper to draw pictures, photos from the internet, etc.

21st Century skills **Get creative**

Telling a short story about something that happened to you during the week will make your vlog fun to watch. Read your notes in Step 2. What would make the best story? Is it funny / scary / silly?

DO

Step 4 **Plan your vlog**

- Look at the storyboard for Lily and James' vlog below.
- Decide how you can use photos, drawings or video clips of people and places in your vlog.
- Use these ideas to plan your storyboard.

Step 5 **Write the script for your vlog**

- Write the introduction for your vlog.
- Write the script for each day of your vlog. Use past tenses and the **Useful language** box to help you.
- Give your script to another student to check your grammar.

Step 6 **Create your vlog**

- Make video clips, find photos and draw the pictures that you need. Practise your script with your partner.
- Record your vlog at school or at home, using your script.
- Show your vlog to your class.

REFLECT

Step 7 **Evaluate the projects**

- Watch all the vlogs. What did you like about them? Which one had the best story?
- Choose one of the vlogs. Think of three questions you want to ask the vloggers about the things they did last week.

Step 8 **Reflect**

- Think about your own project. Is there anything you can improve?

Useful language

Talking about your week

I hardly ever cook. / My mum always pays me.
He was fine. / We weren't scared.
On Monday, we had ... / On Saturday night, I ...
I did chores. / We watched a horror film. / I fell over.
When I was going to school ... / reading a story ...

Asking questions

What did you do? / Did you go out? / Was that ...? / What happened next?

Telling stories

You aren't going to believe this, but ...
I was (going to school) when ...
No way! / You're kidding! / That sounds great.

1 **Hi, everyone. Welcome to our vlog! This is a week in the lives of Lily and James. Here's what we did last week.**

2

Lily: On Monday, we had a Science exam.

James: It was terrible! I didn't revise enough!

3

James: Tuesday was better. After school, I made pasta for dinner. I hardly ever cook, but my whole family loved it, so I was very pleased.

Lily: That sounds great.

James: And my brother tidied the kitchen!

4

Lily: You aren't going to believe this, but when I was going to school on Wednesday, a cat ran out in front of me and I fell over.

James: No way! What did you do?

Lily: All my school books fell out of my bag, so I quickly picked them up and ran to school.

James: Was the cat OK?

Lily: Yeah, he was fine!

5

James: Then it was Thursday. George came to my house and we played computer games.

6

Lily: What did you do on Friday, James? Did you go out after school?

James: No, I did chores for my mum from 3.30 to 5.00 p.m. I took out the recycling and cleaned the whole bathroom.

Lily: Well done, you!

James: My mum always pays me.

7

Lily: And finally – the weekend! On Saturday night, I babysat for my little cousin, Charlotte.

James: Was that an easy job?

Lily: NO! When I was reading a story, Charlotte told me it was boring! And she didn't want to go to sleep.

James: You're kidding!

8

Lily: Yesterday was Sunday. In the evening, we went to the cinema.

James: We watched a horror film.

Lily: But it wasn't very scary. We weren't scared.

James: That's the end of our vlog.

Lily and James: We hope you enjoyed it. Bye!

PROJECT UNITS 4–6

TASK

Create a board game

I can work in a group and produce a language revision board game.

PREPARE

1 Talk about something you've taught yourself to do.

2 Name five health problems in 30 seconds.

3 Say one thing you are doing and one thing you are not doing this weekend.

4 Talk about people you know using superlatives. Use these adjectives: *funny, tall, friendly, intelligent.*

5 Your friend wants to buy a new mobile phone. Give him/her some advice.

6 Finish this sentence. *My parents … , if … .*

7 Name five money verbs. Choose one verb and ask your partner a question.

?

Step 1 **Get ideas**

› Look at the squares above from a board game. Match 1–7 to the correct row in the table in Step 2.

› Which grammar and vocabulary areas from Units 4–6 are not represented in the squares?

Step 2 **Choose your ideas**

	Your ideas
Comparatives	
Giving advice	
If … sentences	
Future plans and predictions	
Reflexives	
Superlatives	
some, any, much, many	
Vocabulary topics	

› Write one or two ideas of your own from Units 4–6 for each category.

› Work in small groups. Discuss which ideas to choose for your board game.

21st Century skills **Think critically**

This board game is for English practice. Which of these questions is better?

1 Which is the best pet – a cat or a dog?

2 Compare a cat and a dog in three different ways.

Step 3 **Do your research**

› Read instruction booklets for board games. What makes a good game?

› Look at different board games online. What makes them look good?

Look! **Teamwork**

Organize your group. You will need to find or draw pictures, write instructions, write text for the squares and design the board. How will you divide the work?

DO

Step 4 **Plan your board game**

- Look at the board game below and create a sketch of your board.
- Decide how many squares you need.
- Use the prompts or think of your own questions.

Step 5 **Write the text and the instructions for your board game**

- Decide on the rules for your game and write simple instructions.
- Write the text for each square on your board. Look at the **Useful language** box to help you.
- Give your text to another student to check your spelling and punctuation.

Step 6 **Create your board game**

- Make your board game.
- Collect the things you need to play the game, for example, a dice and counters.
- Play the board game with your classmates.

REFLECT

Step 7 **Evaluate the projects**

- Which board looks the best? Why?
- Which of the games did you enjoy playing? Why?
- Listen to your classmates' feedback on your game.

Step 8 **Reflect**

- Think about your own board game and your classmates' feedback. Is there anything you can improve?

Useful language

Writing the board squares

Finish this sentence, ...
Compare X and Y
Talk about ... / Tell us about ...
Choose / Name ...
Make two questions using ...
Write a positive and a negative sentence using ...

Grammar

X is more interesting than Y. / X is funnier than Y.
Z is the biggest. / Z is the most exciting.
If it rains tomorrow, I'll ...
I'm meeting my friend after school. / I'm going to order pizza for dinner.
Maybe you should ... / Why don't you ...?

Let's play!

Instructions

Players move down the board from START to FINISH. Use a coin or counter for each person. When it is your turn, move to the next square. Do what the square tells you to do. If your grammar is correct, you will get another turn. 🙂. (Move to the next square and do what it tells you to do.). If your grammar isn't correct, you won't get another turn. ☹️

The player who arrives on the FINISH square first is the winner.

PROJECT UNITS 7–9

TASK

Create a poster presentation about your school year

I can work in pairs and create a poster.

PREPARE

a

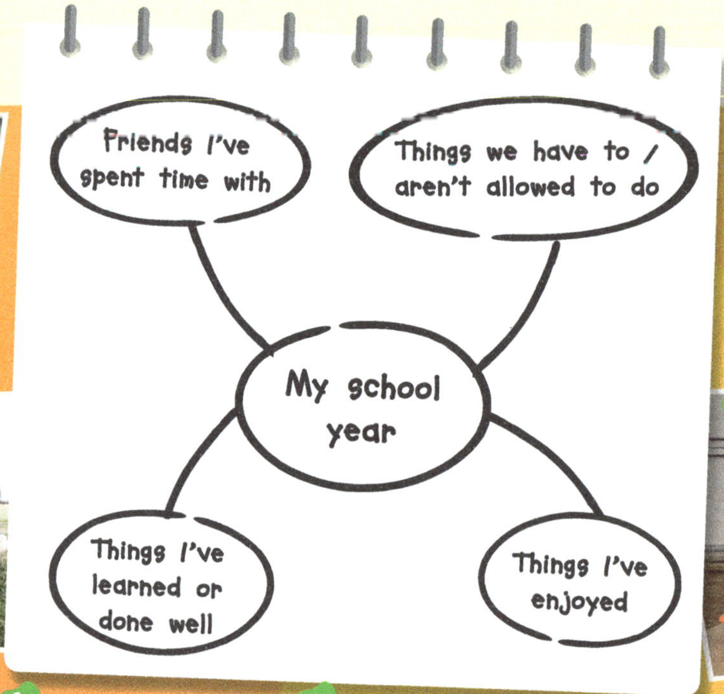

b

c

d

e

f

g

h

Step 1 **Get ideas**

- Look at the photos. What does each photo show?
- Work in pairs. Which photos belong to which category in the mind map?

Step 2 **Choose your ideas**

- Copy the mind map and complete it with your own ideas about your school year.
- Try to remember how you felt about some of the experiences you have had.
- Work in pairs. Compare your lists and share your ideas.
- Together, choose ideas for your poster.

21st Century skills Find out

To help you remember all the things that happened in your school year, check your school website for news and important dates. Looking at photos you have taken on your phone will also remind you of experiences you have had.

Step 3 **Do your research**

- Ask your classmates about experiences/events at your school. Find out how they felt about them and what they learned from them.
- What photos do you need for your poster? Take photos around the school and at home, if you need to.

Look! Cooperation

Sometimes it's hard to think of a lot of ideas. By working together and sharing your ideas, you will have a lot more to choose from for your project.

DO

Step 4 **Plan your poster**

- Think about how many different things you will put on your poster.
- Plan the poster and make a sketch of how the photos and text will look.

Step 5 **Write the text for your poster**

- Write the text for each photo. Use the **Useful language** box to help you.
- Give your text to another student to check your grammar and spelling.

Step 6 **Create and display your poster**

- Put your photos and text together.
- Give your poster a title.
- Display your poster for your class to read.

REFLECT

Step 7 **Evaluate the projects**

- Look at all the posters. Which poster has the best design? Why?
- Say which poster you think is the most interesting to read and why.

Step 8 **Reflect**

- Think about the feedback. Is there anything you can improve?

Useful language

I've done lots of exciting things.
I've been to .../seen/tried ...
It was amazing/scary/fun!
I was very disappointed/embarrassed/surprised/pleased.
I've got better at ...
I used to ..., but now ...
You don't have to ...
We all have to ...
We aren't allowed to ...

My epic school year– by Ella Sanchez

SCHOOL WORK

I've done well in Maths this year. I used to get around 60%, but I've worked really hard and my scores have got better. I feel more confident now in Maths.

FRIENDS

This is my new friend, Nora. We've been friends since September when we first sat together in Science. Nora's very good at Science and she's helped me a lot. She's also very cheerful and funny. She makes me laugh a lot.

FIRST TIME ACTIVITIES

I've done two things this year for the very first time ... .

Drama: I took part in the school musical, which was *Oliver*. I've never sung on stage before. I was surprised that I enjoyed it. It was terrifying, but fun.

Sport: I joined the basketball team. I've only played in one match so far and we lost, so I was very disappointed. However, the team has won more matches this year than last year, so that's good.

SCHOOL RULES

Have you ever seen shoes like this? They're so horrible! I'm embarrassed every day. This year we aren't allowed to wear trainers. We all have to wear black lace-up shoes. I hate them!

CHARITY EVENTS

I've baked a lot of cakes and cookies this year, but I haven't eaten many! A group of my friends decided to raise some money for charity, so for the last six months we've had a cake sale at school every two weeks. Everyone loves cake, so we've raised about £250. We're really pleased about that.

LITERATURE
UNITS 1–3

BEFORE YOU READ

1 Work in pairs. Are you scared of any of the things in the pictures? Why/Why not?

a 
b 
c 
d 

OUTLINE

Oscar

It's the 1930s. Mr Felberg is a tailor, which means he makes clothes for men. He has a shop in a small town in England. Sidney and Joseph work for Mr Felberg. They're learning to be tailors. Sidney is twenty. Joseph is only fifteen and is new at the shop. He's honest and wants to learn.

Sidney isn't honest. He tries to make Joseph look bad in front of Mr Felberg, and sometimes he takes money from the till. He also makes Mr Felberg think he forgets things.

There's an old dummy in the shop called Oscar. Mr Felberg sometimes uses it when he makes clothes. Sidney doesn't like Oscar. He thinks that Oscar can see him when he takes money from the till, and one afternoon he's sure that Oscar hits him. Sidney decides to go to the shop late at night to do something bad to Oscar.

2 Read the outline of *Oscar*. Choose the correct answers.

1 Mr Felberg's shop sells *men's* / *children's* clothes.
2 Sidney and Joseph *are* / *want to be* tailors.
3 Joseph is *older* / *younger* than Sidney.
4 *Sidney* / *Joseph* isn't very nice to Mr Felberg.
5 Sidney thinks that Oscar is *funny* / *real*.

READ

3 L1 Look at the picture. Read and listen to the extract from *Oscar* and answer the questions.

1 Who are the two figures in the picture?
2 Where are they?
3 What's happening? Why?

It was midnight. The street was dark and quiet. Sidney put his key into the shop door. He opened the door. He looked up and down the street. Then he went quickly and quietly into the dark shop.

He waited for a moment.

'Can I do it?' he thought. 'I must do it!'

He saw Oscar. The dummy was in a grey suit now. Sidney moved slowly across the shop, his hands in front of him.

The dummy watched him, its eyes moving.

Sidney put his hands on the dummy. 'Do it!' he said. 'Do it!'

He was afraid, but he carried the dummy across the shop. He carried it through the back room and across to the top of the cellar stairs. Now Sidney looked at the dummy and smiled. 'What am I going to do with you?' he said. 'Do you know?' He laughed. 'I'm going to push you down these stairs!'

He looked at the dummy's face. The dummy's eyes looked back at him. The eyes were hard and black. There was life in those eyes. Once again, Sidney thought, 'This is not only a dummy! It's something … real!'

'No!' he shouted. 'I must not think that!'

He began to push the dummy – but then, suddenly, the dummy began to push Sidney!

'No!' Sidney shouted. 'No, no! Stop! Please ...!'

Then Sidney began to fall down the stairs.

The last thing he saw was Oscar's face ... laughing at him. Then he hit his head on the bottom stair, and everything went black.

• • •

Mr Felberg came to the shop early the next morning.

'Where is Oscar?' he thought.

Joseph came in at that moment.

'Good morning, Mr Felberg,' he said.

'Good morning, Joseph,' Mr Felberg said. 'Where is Oscar? Do you know?'

'No,' Joseph said, surprised.

They walked into the back room – and saw Oscar at the top of the cellar stairs.

'What ...?' Mr Felberg began.

'Look!' Joseph said. 'Oscar is ... smiling!'

It was true. There was a big smile on the dummy's face.

They went quickly across to the cellar stairs and looked down.

Extract from **Richmond Readers**:
Oscar by John Escott

4 Read the extract again. Put the events in the correct order.

a ... Sidney fell down the stairs.
b ... Sidney picked up Oscar and took him to the back of the shop.
c ... Oscar was smiling.
d ... Sidney tried to push Oscar down the stairs.
e ... They found Sidney.
f ... Mr Felberg and Joseph went into the shop.
g ... Sidney went into the shop.

5 Word Power Find three verbs in the text that describe how people communicate. Match them with the meanings. How many more verbs like this can you think of?

1 speak words
2 make sounds when you find something funny
3 speak very loudly

6 L2 Look at the picture and listen to the next part of the story. Are the sentences true (T) or false (F)? Correct the false sentences.

1 Mr Felberg thought Sidney had a broken arm.
2 Mr Felberg didn't believe that Oscar pushed Sidney down the stairs.
3 Sidney left his job at Mr Felberg's shop after the accident.
4 Mr Felberg put Oscar back in the shop window.
5 Joseph was very happy working in the shop after Sidney left.

REFLECT

7 FIND OUT Work in groups. *Oscar* is the story of a dummy that comes to life. Can you find some famous examples of books and films that tell the story of dummies, toys, statues, puppets or other human figures that come to life?

Glossary

suit a formal set of clothes, usually a jacket, and trousers or a skirt, made of the same material
cellar an underground room

LITERATURE UNITS 4–6

BEFORE YOU READ

1 **SPEAKING** **Work in pairs and answer the questions.**

1 What kinds of things do shops do to stop people from stealing their products?
2 What do you think is the best way to stop people from stealing from shops?
3 How do you feel about people who steal things from shops?

OUTLINE

The Detective

When Peter started his new job, he told everybody that he was a detective. But he didn't work for the police, and he wasn't a private detective. He was a store detective for a supermarket – he walked around the shop and looked for people who were trying to steal something.

One morning, Peter saw an old man in the drinks section of the shop. It was a hot day, but the old man was wearing a big coat. Peter thought that the old man was a thief and decided to watch him.

Peter moved so the old man couldn't see him, and he watched him. Soon, the man picked up something expensive. Peter thought he was going to steal it and became excited.

2 **Read the outline of *The Detective*. Are the sentences true (T) or false (F)? Correct the false sentences.**

1 Peter worked for the police.
2 His job was to stop people taking things from a supermarket without paying.
3 Peter believed an old man with a big coat wanted to steal something.

READ

3 L3 **Look at the picture. Read and listen to the extract from *The Detective* and answer the questions.**

1 Who is the young man in the background?
2 What does he think the young woman is doing?
3 What does he do next?

THE DETECTIVE

Suddenly a young woman walked in front of the old man and stopped by one of the shelves. Now Peter couldn't see what the old man was doing. He looked around for somewhere else to stand. There wasn't anywhere. He looked at the girl angrily. And then she took a packet of tea from a shelf and calmly put it in the pocket of her jacket. Peter felt very excited again. 'She's going to steal that packet of tea,' he thought to himself. He forgot all about the old man and went to stand by the main door.

After about five minutes, the girl went past the check-out without paying for the tea. She walked towards the exit.

Peter stepped forward. 'Excuse me, young woman,' he said in an important voice. The girl stopped. 'I'd like you to come with me to the manager's office.'

The girl smiled. 'Why?' she asked. 'Is he going to offer me a job?'

Peter was surprised. Usually people were afraid when he stopped them. This girl seemed calm and relaxed. 'No, he's not going to offer you a job,' he said seriously. 'And this situation is not funny.'

They went to the manager's office. The manager – a short, fat man with a round face – was sitting at his desk. When Peter and the girl walked into the room he stood up.

The girl smiled at him. 'This man said you wanted to offer me a job,' she said.

'I did not,' Peter said angrily. 'I saw this person take a packet of tea from one of the shelves. She put the tea in the pocket of her jacket. Then she tried to walk out of the shop without paying for it.'

The manager looked at the girl and his face became serious. 'Please put everything from your pockets on the desk,' he said.

The girl pulled the packet of tea from her pocket and put it down in front of the manager. She was still smiling.

The manager was surprised. 'Do you agree that you took this tea from a shelf and tried to leave the shop without paying for it?' he asked.

'Of course. I'm not stupid.'

Extract from **Richmond Readers**: *The Road Through the Hills and Other Stories* by Rod Smith

4 Read the extract again. Choose the correct answer.

1 The young woman took a packet of tea and ...
   a put it in her shopping bag.
   b put it in her pocket.
2 Peter stopped the young woman ...
   a before she left the shop.
   b outside the shop.
3 Peter took her to speak to ...
   a the police.
   b the shop manager.
4 The manager asked the girl to ...
   a empty her pockets.
   b explain what she was doing in the shop.
5 The young woman thought the situation was ...
   a funny.
   b frightening.
6 The young woman told the men that she ...
   a drank a lot of tea.
   b took the tea and didn't pay for it.

5 Word Power Find the verbs in the extract and match them with the prepositions a–e. Can you find some other prepositions that can follow the verb 'walk'?

1 look	a up
2 walk	b forward
3 stand	c down
4 put	d out
5 step	e around

6 L4 Listen to the next part of the story. Copy and complete the sentences with the correct words.

1 The girl bought the tea on a ... last week.
2 She took it into the supermarket to compare the ... and ... .
3 The manager was ... with Peter because of the mistake.
4 After she left the supermarket, the girl got into a ... .
5 The driver of the car was the girl's ... .
6 The man had lots of ... and ... inside his coat.

REFLECT

7 THINK CRITICALLY Work in pairs. Discuss the questions about the story.

1 Why do you think the people in the story stole things from the supermarket?
2 What do you think should happen to people who do this?
3 Do you think it is always wrong to steal? Why/Why not?

Glossary

check-out the place in a shop where you pay for the products
exit the door or place where you leave a building
pocket the part of a coat, jacket or pair of trousers that you keep things in

LITERATURE
UNITS 7–9

BEFORE YOU READ

1 SPEAKING Work in pairs and answer the questions.

1 How often are there big storms in your country?
2 Do they ever damage buildings, cars or roads?
3 Have you ever been outside during a big storm? If so, what happened?

OUTLINE

Saturday Storm

Philip (or Phil, for short) is seventeen. He doesn't get on very well with his family and often argues with his dad, Jim, and his sixteen-year-old sister, Viki. He also has a brother, Alex, who's only seven. Phil's family doesn't have much money and in the evenings his mum works as a cleaner to make extra money.

Phil loves playing basketball. He plays in the school team with two of his friends, Steve and Chris. There's a big game in another town on Saturday, and Luke, the team's new trainer, wants them to win. At the team's training session on Thursday, he asks Jim and some of the other parents for money. He says it's to pay for the bus, the court and the referee.

On Saturday, Luke and the team drive to the match in a minibus. Jim, Phil, Viki and Alex follow them in Jim's car. As they drive through the mountains, there's a terrible storm. Suddenly, hundreds of rocks start falling on to the road. They hit the minibus and Jim's car.

2 Read the outline of *Saturday Storm*. Copy and complete the sentences with the correct words.

1 Jim is Phil's … .
2 Phil is in the school … team.
3 … is the new trainer of the team.
4 Luke wants some of the parents to give him some … .
5 On the way to the basketball match, some … hit the bus and car.

READ

3 L5 Look at the picture. Read and listen to the extract from *Saturday Storm* and answer the questions.

1 Who are the people outside the car?
2 What are they trying to do?
3 Who is inside the car?
4 How do you think all the people are feeling?

Jim turned and looked at his children. Philip was badly hurt. There was blood on his face and his arm looked broken. He was covered in rocks and dirt. His eyes were shut and he was not moving.

When Jim turned round to Viki she looked back at him. Her eyes and her mouth were wide open. 'Are you all right?' he asked. She moved her head to say yes.

Jim looked at Alex. He could only see the boy's back. Alex had turned away from the window and pushed his face into the seat. There were rocks and glass and dirt all over him.

'Alex?' Jim said. 'Are you OK?'

Alex moved a little. 'Yes, I think so,' he said. 'Has it stopped?'

'Yes, it has.'

'What happened?'

'It was a landslide,' Jim said. 'Viki, Philip is badly hurt and we must get help very soon.' Jim's voice was very quiet. His face was white. He moved some of the dirt and rocks from Philip's jacket. He put his head down and listened for Philip's heart.

Viki said in a very small voice, 'Is Phil …?'

'No, he's not dead. I can hear his heart,' Jim said. 'I'm going to get out and see what's happening. I want you to help Alex get out and see if he's hurt. Then stay with Phil. I'll be back soon.'

'OK,' Viki said. She opened her door slowly. The car was very near to the side of the road. She could see the sea crashing on the rocks below.

'Come on, Alex,' she said. 'You'll have to be careful. We might fall into the sea from here.'

Alex moved along the seat. Dirt and glass fell off his back. He got out and looked out at the sea. 'Ooh … we're lucky the car didn't go over.' He and Viki got round to the other side of the car.

'We must try to get some of these rocks away from the doors,' she said. 'We can't help Phil until we can open his door.' The two children started moving rocks in the rain.

Jim ran over the top of the fallen rocks to the driver. He could only see some hair. He carefully began to move the rocks. The driver suddenly made a noise. Now Jim could see him. The rain was washing away the dirt from his face.

'Are you all right?' Jim asked.

Extract from **Richmond Readers**: *Saturday Storm* by Julia Newsome

Glossary

blood the red liquid inside our bodies
dirt a substance from the ground or earth that covers things and makes them dirty
landslide earth and rocks that fall down the side of a mountain
rocks large stones

4 Read the extract again. Choose the correct answer.

1 After the landslide, Jim could see that Phillip …
   a was looking at him.
   b was trying to say something.
   c needed to go to hospital.
2 Viki and Alex …
   a couldn't speak, but could move.
   b could speak and move.
   c couldn't move.
3 Jim got out of the car because …
   a he wanted to get help.
   b he wanted to see what happened.
   c it was dangerous to stay in the car.
4 When he got out of the car, Alex felt lucky that …
   a the rocks didn't hit them.
   b the car didn't fall on them.
   c the car wasn't in the sea.
5 Jim climbed over rocks to …
   a speak to the driver of the minibus.
   b look for help.
   c see if the road was open.

5a Word Power Copy and complete the expressions with *get* or *make* from the text.

1 'Philip is badly hurt and we must get … very soon.'
2 'I want you to help Alex get … and see if he's hurt.'
3 'The driver suddenly made … .'

5b Copy and complete the sentences with the correct form of *get* or *make* to make more expressions. Can you think of any other expressions with *get* or *make*?

1 He … a big mistake when he went walking in the mountains at night.
2 Alice and Joe … married in Valencia last summer.
3 I helped my dad to … a cake for my sister's birthday.
4 The boys … bored when it rains because they can't go out.
5 Did you … any friends when you went on holiday?

6 L6 Listen to the next part of the story. Put the events in order from 1–6.

a … Steve went to help the driver of the bus.
b … Luke tried to phone someone.
c … Jim became angry with Luke.
d … Luke got out of the bus.
e … Chris tried to phone the emergency services.
f … Jim pushed Luke and took his phone.

REFLECT

7 GET CREATIVE Work in pairs. Think about how Jim and Luke behaved in the story. Then act out a conversation between Jim and Luke on the day after the accident.

EXAM PRACTICE
UNIT 1

SPEAKING
Discussion

Look! About the task

In this speaking task, you will talk with your partner about some pictures. The examiner will then ask you some more questions about the topic.

Useful strategies

- Listen carefully to the questions your partner, or the examiner, is asking.
- Don't just answer 'yes' or 'no', but give reasons for your answer.
- Try to give a long answer using two or three sentences.

1 **Match questions 1–5 with answers a–e. Compare with a partner.**

1 Do you like watching horror films?
2 Where do you usually watch films?
3 Are you learning karate?
4 How often do you go to a museum?
5 Do you enjoy going to the zoo?

a At home. I download them from the internet.
b Yes, I do. I love seeing the animals.
c No, they're scary! I enjoy science-fiction films.
d Yes, I am. It's brilliant!
e I sometimes go with my dad to see exhibitions.

2 **Think of some questions to ask about free-time activities. Here are some ideas to help you. Discuss with a partner.**

What's your favourite ...?
When do you usually ...?
Do you enjoy ...?
Where do you and your family/friends ...?
How often do you ...?

3 E1.1 **Listen to two dialogues about free-time activities. Say which dialogue is better and why. Discuss with a partner.**

4 **Look at the pictures and questions in the EXAM TASK.**

EXAM TASK

Ask and answer these questions with your partner.

1 Which of these activities do you like doing in your free time? Why?
2 Which of these activities do you like doing best? Why?
3 Do you think visiting museums is boring? Why/Why not?
4 How often do you cook?
5 Do you prefer eating at home or eating in restaurants? Why?
6 Do you prefer playing computer games or being outside? Why?

a

b

c

d

e

5 E1.2 **Now listen to a student answering the examiner's questions. How were his answers different from yours? Discuss with a partner.**

EXAM PRACTICE UNIT 2

LISTENING
Multiple choice

Look! **About the task**

In this listening task, you will hear five short dialogues relating to five questions. You must read each question, listen to the dialogue and choose from pictures A–C. Each dialogue is played twice.

Useful strategies

- Before you listen, read the question and look at the three pictures underneath it. Think about the types of words you are going to hear.
- You will hear something about <u>all</u> the pictures for each question. Listen for the whole meaning, not just individual words.

1 **Look at the pictures in question 1 of the EXAM TASK. Which of the following phrases do you think you will hear while you are listening?**

clean the bathroom   do the laundry
do the shopping   do the washing up
tidy my room   wash the floor

2 **Now look at the pictures in questions 2–5 of the EXAM TASK. Which words do you think you will hear? Discuss with a partner.**

3 E2.1 **Look at question 1 of the EXAM TASK again. Read and listen to the conversation. Which is the correct answer? Why?**

Mum: Leo, can you do some chores today, please?
Leo: OK, Mum. I'm going to tidy my room this afternoon. It's a real mess!
Mum: It certainly is! Before you do that, can you do the laundry?
Leo: Sure. What else would you like me to do?
Mum: Well, you can wash the kitchen floor, as well. But do that this evening after dinner, please. OK?
Leo: OK.

4 **Now complete the EXAM TASK.**

EXAM TASK

E2.2 For each question, listen and choose the correct picture.

1 Which chore will the boy do first?

A

B

C

2 When does the film start?

A

B

C

3 Where was the girl at the weekend?

A

B

C

4 What job does the boy's uncle do?

A

B

C

5 How much was the girl's T-shirt?

A

B

C

EXAM PRACTICE
UNIT 3

WRITING
Picture story

Look! **About the task**

In this writing task, you will write a story of at least 35 words. You will have three pictures to help you write your story.

Useful strategies

- Organize your story into paragraphs. Start a new paragraph for each picture.
- Make your story interesting by using past simple and continuous tenses, time expressions and adjectives.
- When you finish, check your spelling and grammar.

1 **Look at the pictures below and answer the questions.**

1 What are the people doing?
2 Which animals can you see?
3 Are the people safe or are they in danger? Why?

a

b

c

2 **Read the Useful Strategies box again. Read Stefano and Carla's stories. Which story is better? Why? Discuss with a partner.**

<u>Stefano</u>

Last month, Harry and Jodie visited the jungle.

They saw lots of interesting animals there. While they were exploring, Harry took some photos of a small monkey. The monkey was sitting in a tree.

While Harry was taking photos, Jodie heard a noise. She saw a huge snak and it was moving along the ground! Jodie said, 'Don't move Harry. There's a snak near you.'

Harry picked up a piece of wood and throw it to the snake. Then Harry and Jodie ran away.

(84 words)

<u>Carla</u>

Harry and Jodie was visiting the jungel in Brazil when they were seeing a sneke. Harry was throwing one wood at it and they running away. They were afraid.

(29 words)

3 **Now complete the EXAM TASK.**

EXAM TASK

Look at the three pictures. Write the story shown in the pictures. Write 35 words or more.

a

b

c

EXAM PRACTICE UNIT 4

SPEAKING
Conversation

Look! **About the task**

In this speaking task, you will have a conversation with the examiner about a topic for two minutes. You will answer questions on the topic, and you must also ask the examiner some questions.

Useful strategies

- Listen carefully to the examiner's questions – these may be in the present tense, the past tense or the future tense.
- Remember to continue the conversation by asking the examiner a different question about the topic.
- Use different question words (*who*, *what*, *why*, *where*, *when*, *how*) and tenses.

1 Match questions 1–6 with answers a–f. Compare with a partner.

1 How often do you buy new clothes?
2 Who do you go shopping with?
3 When did you last buy a present for someone?
4 How much money did you spend when you last went shopping?
5 Where are you going to go shopping?
6 What do you like buying?

a I think I spent about £15.
b I love buying electronic gadgets.
c Around two or three times a month.
d I usually go with my mum, but sometimes with my sister.
e I'm going to go to the supermarket for food.
f I got my friend a computer game for his birthday.

2 E4.1 You are going to listen to two teenagers talking about shopping. Read the statements below. Which do you think the speakers will do? Listen and check.

- only give 'Yes' or 'No' answers
- explain their reasons
- both ask questions
- disagree with each other
- give details in their answers
- use different tenses

3 Now talk about shopping. Look at the question prompts. Student A asks the questions, and Student B answers. At the end, Student B asks one 'new' question.

1 Do you enjoy ...?
2 Have you ever bought anything ...?
3 What do people usually buy in ...?
4 When did you last go to a ...?
5 How much pocket money do you ...?
6 Which is better: paying in cash or ...?

4 Complete the EXAM TASK.

EXAM TASK

Work with your partner again, but change roles.

Where does your family buy food?
Is it better to buy vegetables in a shop, or from a market?
When did you last go to a supermarket?
What did you buy in the supermarket?
Where will you have lunch today?
What will you have?

5 E4.2 Now listen to two students doing the EXAM TASK. How was your conversation different? Discuss with your partner.

EXAM PRACTICE UNIT 5

READING
Multiple-choice gap fill

Look! About the task

In this reading task, you will read a short text and choose the correct words (a, b or c) to fill in the gaps.

Useful strategies

- First, read the whole text to understand what it is about.
- Look carefully at the words before and after the gap. These may help you decide which word best fits.
- Remember that only one answer is correct.

1 Look at the following sentences and choose the correct answer.

1 Both my brothers enjoy *eating* / *catching* fish and chips.
2 Teenagers shouldn't *go* / *stay* up late every night.
3 If we don't drink enough water, we can *catch* / *get* a headache.
4 What's the *matter* / *wrong* with you?
5 Lisa gave me a top *tip* / *advice* for studying English.

2 Read the text. Choose the correct answer to complete the text.

BEING VEGAN

Eleni Loukas is a vegan, which means she doesn't eat any animal products such as meat, dairy or eggs. Many people [1]... this a 'plant-based diet' instead of a vegan diet. As well as only eating plants, some vegans don't wear any clothes that are [2]... from animal products, such as leather shoes or woollen jumpers.

Eleni [3]... to become a vegan because she wanted to eat more healthily. She also cares about what is happening to the planet.

1	a say	b call	c think
2	a changed	b built	c made
3	a guessed	b decided	c explained

3 Look again at the options for gaps 1-3 in the text in Exercise 2. Decide why the other answers are wrong. Discuss with a partner.

4 Now complete the EXAM TASK.

EXAM TASK

Choose the correct options to complete the text.

How to be healthy at any age

It's important to eat plenty of fruit and vegetables – we get useful vitamins and minerals from these foods. And we shouldn't eat too much sugar. Sugar is in a lot of different food, [1]... biscuits, cakes and drinks. We should also drink around eight glasses of water [2]... day. Water is good for our skin, and when we are thirsty, it's the [3]... thing to drink.

Doing sport is a good way to [4]... our bodies fit. Team sports, such as basketball, are fun. If you don't enjoy team sports, you can [5]... for a run or a bike ride.

We should also get [6]... sleep every night because sleep is good for our brains. Teenagers, for example, should sleep for around nine hours. Small changes to our lifestyle can make a big difference.

1	a around	b like	c without
2	a most	b another	c every
3	a best	b fine	c excellent
4	a keep	b have	c improve
5	a do	b make	c go
6	a several	b enough	c any

EXAM PRACTICE UNIT 6

LISTENING
Matching

Look! About the task

In this listening task, you will listen to a conversation between two people and match the names to the items mentioned. Each conversation is played twice.

Useful strategies

- Read the instructions carefully to understand what the conversation will be about.
- Then, read the words in the two lists carefully. There will be more words in the list of items (on the right) than you need.
- The first time you listen, get an idea of what the conversation is about and choose your answer.
- The second time you listen, check your answers carefully.

1 E6.1 **Listen to a conversation about a birthday party. What will each person buy for the party? Choose the correct answers.**

1 Charlie
2 Clara
3 Uncle Mike

a pizza
b snacks
c balloons

2 E6.1 **Listen again and answer the questions. Compare with a partner.**

1 Where are Zoe's family coming from?
2 What kind of pizza will everyone eat?
3 What snacks will Charlie bring?
4 Who is going to make the cake?
5 What is Zoe's favourite cake?

3 Now complete the EXAM TASK.

EXAM TASK

E6.2 Listen to Maddy talking to Harry about a party. What will each person bring to the party?

For each question, choose the correct answer.

1 Sophie	**A** fireworks
2 Paul	**B** games
3 Anna	**C** lights
4 Toby	**D** snacks
5 Ellie	**E** decorations
	F takeaway
	G drinks

4 **Work in pairs. Compare your answers to Exercise 3.**

5 **Which parts of the EXAM TASK did you find easy and which parts did you find difficult? Discuss your answers with a partner.**

EXAM PRACTICE UNIT 7

READING
Multiple choice

Look! About the task

In this reading task, you will read a short text in which some words or phrases are missing. For each question, you must choose the correct word or phrase to complete the gap. There will be four choices.

Useful strategies

- Read the whole text before you answer the questions. This will help you understand what it is about.
- Then read each sentence before you decide which word fits in the gap.
- There is only one correct answer.

1 **Read the text below. Decide if a word or a phrase is missing in each gap.**

Hi Emily

How are you? I went to the cinema last night, but I didn't enjoy it at all. Nothing exciting happened in the film and I was so [1] … .

Anyway, we're going skydiving tomorrow! Have you [2] … tried that? I did it last year with my cousin and we [3] … . Would you like to come [4] … us tomorrow?

Let me know.

Ollie

2 **Look at gaps 1 and 3 again. Decide which word or phrase best fits in each gap. Discuss with a partner.**

Gap 1

bored calm confident worried

Gap 3

have such a good time
are having a so good time
had such a good time
had a so good time

3 **Now look at gaps 2 and 4. Think of a word or phrase to fit in each gap. Discuss with a partner.**

4 **Now complete the EXAM TASK.**

EXAM TASK

Choose the correct options to complete the text.

Hi Jack

How are you? I'm on holiday in New Zealand with my family. It's [1] … great country and we're having an amazing time. Yesterday, we took part in a carnival and that was great fun.

Today, we're going to a rock-climbing centre. I [2] … rock climbing before, but my sister has and she loves it. I'm so [3] … about trying it – I can't wait! [4] … been rock climbing? If you have, tell me about it.

I'll email you again tomorrow when I have more time, and I'll send you some photos!

Love

Ben

1 a so a
b a such
c such a
d so

2 a have been
b haven't seen
c have gone
d haven't done

3 a cheerful
b excited
c surprised
d disappointed

4 a Have you ever
b Did you go
c Where did you go
d When did you

EXAM PRACTICE UNIT 8

LISTENING
Multiple choice

Look! About the task

In this listening task, you will hear a conversation between two people and answer five multiple-choice questions. You will hear the conversation twice.

Useful strategies

- Before you listen, read all the instructions. Then read each question and the options carefully to understand what the topic is about.
- Think about the topic and which words or phrases you might hear.
- Listen carefully to check the details
- You will hear some information about all three answers, but only one answer is correct. Listen for the whole meaning.

1 **Read the situations in the EXAM TASK and the list of words and phrases below. Which words and phrases do you think you might hear?**

alone
argue with
be a fan
be kind to
community
famous people
get angry with
get on well with
hang out with
kids
poverty
study
supermarket
walking the dog
with family

2 **Write down some more words and phrases you think you will hear. Discuss with a partner.**

3 **Now complete the EXAM TASK.**

EXAM TASK

E8.1 Listen to Danny talking to Carla about helping people. Choose the correct options.

1 Danny says that Mrs Moore ...
  a doesn't have many friends locally.
  b has always lived on her own.
  c has lived in her house since 2018.
2 Danny says that he enjoys ...
  a making Mrs Moore laugh.
  b doing Mrs Moore's shopping.
  c looking after Mrs Moore's pet.
3 What do Danny and Mrs Moore often do?
  a pick up litter
  b donate blood
  c raise money for charity
4 Next week, Danny is going to ...
  a go to a cake sale.
  b do a charity bike ride.
  c help at the after-school club.
5 In March, Danny and Carla plan to work with ...
  a some celebrities.
  b homeless people.
  c poor children.

EXAM PRACTICE UNIT 9

READING
Short texts

Look! About the task

In this reading task, you will read six short texts and choose one option (a, b or c) which matches the meaning in each text.

Useful strategies

- Before you answer, read each text quickly to understand what it is about.
- Look at all three options before you decide which one is correct.
- Read each option carefully with the text. Only <u>one</u> will have the same meaning as the text.

1 **Read the information below. What is it about?**

2 **Now read the three options: a, b and c. Decide which one is the best summary of the information.**

PETE'S PIZZAS

Buy one, get one free!

Monday – Thursday

5–6 p.m. only

a The pizza shop is open on Mondays and Thursdays.
b Two pizzas cost the same as one on some days.
c Pizzas are free in the afternoons.

3 **Now look at the other two answers. Tell your partner why they are wrong.**

3 **Now complete the EXAM TASK.**

EXAM TASK

Choose the correct option for each text.

1

Hi Marta

Thanks for getting me that book I wanted. I'll pay you for it tomorrow when I see you at school.

Zoe

a Zoe wants Marta to buy her a book.
b Zoe didn't give Marta her book back.
c Zoe will give Marta some money for a book soon.

2

Woodford Zoo

Half-price tickets for all students
Children under eight free

Please ask at the gate.

a Everybody must pay at the gate to go in.
b If you are an adult, it's more expensive to go in.
c There are special activities for very young children.

3

Mark

I'm at the dentist's with your sister, so I won't be at the school gates at 3.30. Please catch the bus today.

Mum

a Mark's mum is telling him how to get home.
b Mark's mum is telling him to meet her at the dentist's.
c Mark's mum is explaining to him where he should meet his sister.

4

For sale

Men's red mountain bike - six years old - needs new tyres

Call Steve after 6 p.m. - 07836 689431

a You can speak to the owner of the bicycle in the afternoon.
b The new owner of the bicycle should change the tyres.
c The bicycle for sale used to belong to a child.

5

Practice for school football team in gym today at 4.00 p.m. – football field too wet

a If you are in the school football team, you should go to the gym.
b The football team should meet in the football field.
c The football team will not play today because of the weather.

LANGUAGE SUMMARY

UNIT 1

GRAMMAR

Present simple

Affirmative	Negative
I/You often **read** in bed.	I/You **don't buy** books online.
He/She **watches** a lot of films.	He/She **doesn't like** musicals.
We/You/They **love** comedies.	We/You/They **don't read** comics.
Questions	**Short answers**
Do you **read** on holiday?	Yes, I **do**. / No, I **don't**.
Does he **like** horror films?	Yes, he **does**. / No, he **doesn't**.

Rules

We use the present simple to talk about facts, habits and routines.

Adverbs and expressions of frequency

I'm **never** late for school.
She **sometimes** plays tennis.
We clean our teeth **twice a day**.
The Olympics take place **every four years**.

Rules

We use adverbs and expressions of frequency with the present simple to say how often we do things.

Adverbs of frequency include: *always, usually, often, sometimes, hardly ever, never*. They go after the verb *be*, but before other verbs.

Expressions of frequency include: *once/twice a day/week/month, every day/two weeks*, etc. They usually go at the end of a sentence.

Present continuous

Affirmative	Negative
I'**m waiting** for a friend.	I'**m not wearing** a coat.
He/She'**s making** a cake.	He/She **isn't talking**.
You/We/They'**re dancing**.	You/We/They **aren't driving**.
Questions	**Short answers**
Are you **watching** TV?	Yes, I **am**. / No, I'**m not**.
Is he **sleeping**?	Yes, he **is**. / No, he **isn't**.

Rules

We use the present continuous to talk about actions in progress now.

Present simple and present continuous

Present simple	Present continuous
I often **download** films.	I'**m downloading** a film now.

Rules

We use the present simple to talk about facts, habits and routines.

We use the present continuous to talk about actions in progress now.

VOCABULARY

Types of film

action film
animated film
comedy
documentary
drama
fantasy film
historical film
horror film
musical
science-fiction film

Adjectives to describe films

boring
brilliant
confusing
enjoyable
exciting
funny
romantic
sad
scary
serious
silly
terrible

SPEAKING

Making and responding to suggestions

What shall we do this afternoon/tomorrow?
How about / What about ...?
Why don't we ...?
I'm not sure.
That sounds scary/boring/exciting.
I'd prefer to ...
That's fine by me.

WRITING

Reviewing a film

One of my favourite films is ...
The film is set in ...
The actors are ...
The special effects are ...
The plot is simple/confusing.
The ending is exciting/silly.

Writing a conclusion

In conclusion, I recommend it.
In conclusion, I didn't enjoy it at all.

LANGUAGE SUMMARY UNIT 2

GRAMMAR

Past simple

Affirmative	Negative
I/You/He/She/We/They **cleaned** the kitchen.	I/You/He/She/We/They **didn't tidy** her room.
I/You/He/She/We/They **made** dinner.	I/You/He/She/We/They **didn't do** the shopping.
Questions	**Short answers**
Did you **have** lunch?	Yes, I **did**. / No, I **didn't**.
Did it **rain** last night?	Yes, it **did**. / No, it **didn't**.

Rules

We use the past simple to talk about completed actions in the past.

For regular verbs, the past simple affirmative form ends in *-ed*.

A lot of verbs have irregular affirmative forms. The forms are the same for all pronouns.

be: past simple

Affirmative	Negative
I/He/She **was** tired.	I/He/She **wasn't** at school.
You/We/They **were** late.	You/We/They **weren't** happy.
There was a party last night.	**There wasn't** much food.
There were a lot of people at the beach.	**There weren't** any restaurants.
Questions	**Short answers**
Was she a journalist?	Yes, she **was**. / No, she **wasn't**.
Were they farmers?	Yes, they **were**. / No, they **weren't**.
Was there any music?	Yes, there **was**. / No, there **wasn't**.
Were there any cafés at the beach?	Yes, there **were**. / No, there **weren't**.

Rules

We form the past simple of *be* with *was* and *were*.

There was / *there were* are the past simple forms of *there is* / *there are*.

could and *couldn't*

Affirmative	
I/You/He/She/It/We/They **could** walk and talk.	
Negative	
I/You/He/She/It/We/They **couldn't** ride a bike.	
Questions	**Short answers**
Could you play the piano?	Yes, I **could**. / No, I **couldn't**.

Rules

We use *could* and *couldn't* to talk about ability in the past.

VOCABULARY

Jobs around the home

clean the bathroom
do the laundry
do the shopping
do the washing up
lay the table
load the dishwasher
make dinner
make your bed
take out the rubbish/recycling
tidy your room
wash the car
wash the floor

Jobs

dentist
designer
engineer
farmer
journalist
lawyer
mechanic
nurse
personal trainer
police officer
receptionist
shop assistant

SPEAKING

Talking about skills and abilities

Why are you interested in ...?
How well can you ...?
Do you enjoy ...?
Quite well. / Very well. / Not very well.
I'm (not very) good at ...
I love/enjoy ...
I know how to ...

WRITING

Writing about a person's life

He/She was born in ...
He/She died in ...
He/She grew up in/on ...
As a child, he/she ...
He/She went to university in ...
He/She got a job as a ...

Prepositions of time

He studied P.E. **from** 1883 **to** 1887.

His students played football **for** most of the year.

He worked there **until** 1937.

LANGUAGE SUMMARY UNIT 3

GRAMMAR

Past continuous

Affirmative	Negative
I **was working** last night.	I **wasn't doing** my homework.
He/She **was sleeping**.	He/She **wasn't watching** TV.
You/We/They **were eating**.	You/We/They **weren't listening**.
Questions	**Short answers**
Was it **raining** yesterday?	Yes, it **was**. / No, it **wasn't**.
Were they **celebrating**?	Yes, they **were**. / No, they **weren't**.

Rules

We use the past continuous to talk about a long action in progress in the past.

We form the past continuous with the past simple of *be* + verb + *-ing*.

Past simple and past continuous

Jen **was having** dinner **when** her dad **phoned**.
While we **were cycling** in town, we **saw** our friends.

Jen was having dinner
We were cycling in town
now
her dad phoned
we saw our friends

Rules

We use different tenses to talk about a short completed action that interrupts a longer action in progress in the past:

The past continuous describes a longer action that was in progress in the past.

The past simple describes a short action that interrupted the longer action.

We use *when* and *while* to link the two actions:

We often use *when* before the past simple.

We often use *while* before the past continuous.

Past time expressions

We went to the cinema **yesterday afternoon**.
They saw their cousins **the day before yesterday**.
She had a Maths exam **last week**.
I bought a new phone **two weeks ago**.

Rules

We use *yesterday* + *morning* / *afternoon* / *evening* to talk about the day before today. But we say *last night*.

We use *the day before yesterday* to mean two days ago.

We use *last* + *night* / *week* / *month* / *year* to mean the most recent night, week, month or year.

We use a length of time + *ago* to say when in the past something happened.

VOCABULARY

Verbs of movement

climb
crawl
dive
fall
jump
pull
push
run
swim
walk

Prepositions of movement

across
along
around
down
into
off
onto
over
through
up

Adjectives and adverbs

angry – angrily
easy – easily
fast – fast
good – well
happy – happily
hard – hard
hungry – hungrily
loud – loudly
quick – quickly
quiet – quietly
slow – slowly

SPEAKING

Telling a story and reacting

Guess what happened yesterday/ last weekend/on Wednesday!
I was ... when I ...
You aren't going to believe this, but ...
No, really.
No way!
You're kidding!
What happened next?
Wow, that's amazing!

WRITING

Writing a story

Last weekend/month/summer, ...
When we arrived, it was (late).
We were (walking down the path) (slowly) when suddenly ...
While we were (waiting), ...
What a weekend/day/holiday!

when, while, during

We were walking down the path **when** suddenly a man in front of us fell.
While we were waiting, we heard the sound of a helicopter.
During the night, it rained heavily.

LANGUAGE SUMMARY
UNIT 4

GRAMMAR

Quantifiers: *some, any, (how) much, many, a lot of*

Countable nouns	Uncountable nouns
Affirmative	
I bought **some** bananas.	We ate **some** rice.
There were **a lot of** people.	There was **a lot of** traffic.
Negative	
We didn't play **any** games.	We haven't got **any** cheese.
I didn't eat **many** / **a lot of** peas.	There isn't **much** / **a lot of** fruit.
Questions	
Are there **any** oranges?	Have you got **any** money?
Has he got **many** / **a lot of** friends?	Do you do **much** / **a lot of** sport?
How many books have you got?	**How much** food is there?

Rules

We use *some* and *a lot of* in affirmative sentences and we use *any* in negative sentences and questions.

With countable nouns, we use *many* in negative sentences and questions. With uncountable nouns, we use *much* in negative sentences and questions.

We can use *a lot of* in affirmative and negative sentences and in questions.

Comparatives and superlatives

Adjective		Comparative	Superlative
Short	small	small**er**	**the** small**est**
	wet	wet**ter**	**the** wet**test**
	happy	happ**ier**	**the** happ**iest**
Long	comfortable	**more** comfortable	**the most** comfortable
Irregular	good	**better**	**the best**
	bad	**worse**	**the worst**
	far	**further**	**the furthest**

Rules

We use the comparative + *than* to compare two things:
*I'm **taller than** my dad.*

We use *the* + superlative to compare more than two things:
*Delia is **the tallest** student in our class.*

(not) as ... as

These jeans are**n't as cheap as** the ones in the other shop.
Spanish food is **as good as** Italian food.

Rules

We use *not as* + adjective + *as* to compare two things that are different. It has the opposite meaning to a comparative adjective:
I'm not as tall as my brother. = My brother is taller than me.

We use *as* + adjective + *as* to compare two things that are the same:
I'm as tall as my dad.

VOCABULARY

Containers

bag, bottle, bowl, box, can, carton, cup, glass, jar, packet, tin, tube

Money verbs

borrow, buy, cost, earn, lend, pay by card, save, sell, shop online, spend

SPEAKING

Comparing products

What do you think of this one/these ones?
Which colour do you prefer?
It looks/They look ..., but it's/they're ...
The ... is/are much ...
It isn't/They aren't as ... as the ...
You're right.
That's true.
I agree.

WRITING

Survey results

Last week, we did a class survey about ...
Our group interviewed ...
Here are the results.
The most popular answers were ...

Expressions of quantity

Everybody ...
Most students ...
Half of the students ...
Some students ...
A few students ...
A couple of students ...
Nobody ...

LANGUAGE SUMMARY UNIT 5

GRAMMAR

will and *won't*; *may* and *may not*

Affirmative	
I/You/He/She/It/We/They **will know** what to do.	
I/You/He/She/It/We/They **may be** late.	
Negative	
I/You/He/She/We/They **won't understand**.	
I/You/He/She/We/They **may not go** to the party.	
Questions	**Short answers**
Will humans **live** on Mars?	Yes, they **will**. / No, they **won't**.

Rules

We use *will* and *won't* to make predictions about the future.

We use *may* and *may not* when we are not certain about a prediction: *It may rain. = Perhaps it will rain.*

First conditional

Situation	Result
If you **don't hurry**,	you**'ll be** late.
If he **falls** over,	he**'ll hurt** himself.
Result	**Situation**
I**'ll text** you later	if I **have** time.
They**'ll get** wet	if they **go** out now.

Rules

We use the first conditional to talk about situations and their results.

To describe the situation, we use *if* + present simple.

To describe the result, we use *will* or *won't* + infinitive.

We use a comma after the situation if we put it before the result.

should and *shouldn't*

Affirmative	
I/You/She/He/We/They **should** drink lots of water.	
Negative	
I/You/She/He/We/They **shouldn't** go to school.	
Questions	**Short answers**
Should I see a doctor?	Yes, you **should**. / No, you **shouldn't**.

Rules

We use *should* and *shouldn't* to give advice.

After *should*, we use the infinitive of the main verb without *to*.

VOCABULARY

The human body

ankle
bone
brain
elbow
face
finger
heart
knee
neck
shoulder
skin
stomach
throat
thumb
toe

Health problems

I've got a broken leg.
I've got a cold.
I've got a cough.
I've got a headache.
I've got a sore throat.
I've got a stomach ache.
I've got sunburn.
I've got a temperature.
I've got toothache.
My back hurts.

SPEAKING

Giving advice

What's the matter?
What's wrong?
You don't look very well/happy.
Maybe you should ...
You shouldn't ...
Why don't you ...?
I'm sure it'll be OK.

WRITING

Giving tips and advice

Here are (my) top tips for ...
It's important (not) to ...
You should always/never ...
It's a good idea to ...
Remember that ...

Imperatives

Think about what you put online.
Don't accept their request.
Always show respect.
Never meet with someone that you only know online.

LANGUAGE SUMMARY
UNIT 6

GRAMMAR

be going to

Affirmative	Negative
I'**m going to buy** a new phone.	I'**m not going to do** any work.
He/She'**s going to make** a cake.	He/She **isn't going to have** a holiday.
You/We/They'**re going to watch** a film.	You/We/They **aren't going to drive**.
Questions	**Short answers**
Are you **going to hire** a DJ?	Yes, I **am**. / No, I'**m not**.
Is she **going to learn** French?	Yes, she **is**. / No, she **isn't**.

Rules

We use *be going to* to talk about future plans and intentions.

be going to and *will*

We'**re going to go** to the beach tomorrow. Hopefully it'**ll be** sunny.
We'**re going to get** there early. It **will** probably **be** busy.

Rules

We use *be going to* to talk about future plans and intentions.

We use *will* to make predictions about the future.

Present continuous for future arrangements

'What **are** you **doing** tonight?' 'I'**m meeting** some friends in town.'
'**Are** you **going** to the cinema?' 'No, we'**re seeing** a band.'

Rules

We can use the present continuous to talk about arrangements (fixed plans) in the future.

We often use a time expression, for example, *tonight*, *tomorrow*, *next weekend*, *on Saturday*.

Reflexive pronouns

Singular		Plural	
Subject pronoun	Reflexive pronoun	Subject pronoun	Reflexive pronoun
I	**myself**	we	**ourselves**
you	**yourself**	you (plural)	**yourselves**
he	**himself**	they	**themselves**
she	**herself**		
it	**itself**		

Rules

When the same person is the subject and object of a verb, we use a reflexive pronoun:

***He's** teaching **himself** Portuguese.*

subject object

VOCABULARY

Party plans

buy food
buy snacks
choose a date
choose a place
create a playlist
have fun
hire a DJ
order a takeaway
post your party on social media
put up decorations
put up lights
send invitations
write a guest list

Things for a camping trip

first-aid kit
hoodie
phone charger
pillow
raincoat
sleeping bag
soap
sun cream
sunglasses
tent
toothbrush
torch
towel
water bottle

SPEAKING

Asking for and offering help

Could you ...?
Would you mind ...?
Shall I help you?
What can I do to help?
Do you want me to ...?
I'll ...
That would be great/really helpful.

WRITING

Writing a thank-you letter

Dear ...
Thank you for the ... that you sent me.
It was very kind/generous of you.
I had a great/fantastic birthday.
Lots of love / Best wishes

Preposition + *-ing*

They're perfect **for** listen**ing** to music.
I'm thinking **of** us**ing** the money to buy a new bike.

LANGUAGE SUMMARY
UNIT 7

GRAMMAR

Present perfect affirmative and negative

Affirmative
I**'ve travelled** to lots of countries.
He/She**'s won** a competition.
You/We/They**'ve lived** abroad.
Negative
I **haven't seen** a dolphin.
He/She **hasn't ridden** a horse.
You/We/They **haven't eaten** insects.

Rules

We use the present perfect to describe an experience in someone's life. We don't say exactly when the experience happened.

We form the present perfect with the correct form of *have* + past participle.

To form the past participle of regular verbs, we add *-ed* to the verb.

A lot of verbs have irregular past participles. For some verbs, past participles are the same as past simple irregular forms: *buy – bought, bought.*

Sometimes they are different: *take – took, taken*

Present perfect questions; *ever* and *never*

Questions	Short answers
Have you (**ever**) **eaten** octopus?	Yes, I **have**. / No, I **haven't**.
Has he/she (**ever**) **met** any famous actors?	Yes, he/she **has**. / No, he/she **hasn't**.
Have they (**ever**) **climbed** a mountain?	Yes, they **have**. / No, they **haven't**.
Affirmative	
I/You/We/They **have never flown** in a helicopter.	
He/She **has never tried** skydiving.	

Rules

We form questions in the present perfect with *have/has* + subject + past participle.

We often use *ever* with present perfect questions. *Ever* means at any time in your life.

We can also use *never* with the affirmative form of the present perfect. *Never* means at no time in my life.

VOCABULARY

Expressions with *get, go, make* and *take*

get a (good) job
get better (at)
get good marks
go on an adventure
go (scuba diving)
make (new) friends
make (lots of) money
take my driving test
take part (in)

Feelings

angry
bored
calm
cheerful
confident
disappointed
embarrassed
excited
nervous
pleased
scared
surprised
upset
worried

SPEAKING

Asking for and giving information

How can I help you?
I'm interested in ...
Have you tried ... before?
Do I need any special equipment?
The price includes the equipment.
How much is it?
We provide everything.
Is there anything else I need to know?

WRITING

Describing things you've done

We've done lots of exciting things.
We've climbed ... / been to ... / seen ...
It was amazing / great fun!
Tomorrow, we're going to go to ...

so and *such*

It's **so** warm.
I'm having **such** a good time!

LANGUAGE SUMMARY UNIT 8

GRAMMAR

Present perfect with *for* and *since*

for	*since*
I**'ve known** him **for** six months. Julia **hasn't messaged** me **for** a week.	I**'ve known** him **since** December. Julia **hasn't messaged** me **since** last Friday.
Time expressions with *for*	**Time expressions with *since***
five minutes ten days three weeks six months a year a long time ages	twelve o'clock Wednesday the weekend January 2019 I was ten years old last night

Rules

We use the present perfect + *for* or *since* to talk about something that began in the past and is still true now.

We use *for* + a length of time.

We use *since* + a point in time.

Present perfect and past simple

Present perfect	Past simple
I**'ve eaten** snails.	I **ate** them in France **last year**.
They**'ve climbed** Mount Everest.	They **climbed** it **in 2018**.
Have you ever **seen** a lion?	I **saw** a lion **last summer**. I **saw** it at a safari park with my family.
I**'ve stayed** in a five-star hotel.	I **stayed** in the hotel **two years ago**.

Rules

We use the present perfect and the past simple to talk about an experience.

We use the present perfect when we aren't interested in when it happened, only the fact that it happened.

We use the past simple to give more details about an experience. We use it to specify the time when it happened.

We also use it to give information such as where it happened, who you were with, etc.

In a conversation, we use the present perfect to describe an experience, but we usually change to the past simple to ask more questions.

A: *I**'ve met** Lionel Messi.*

B: *Really, how **did** you **meet** him?*

A: *I **met** him at a restaurant in Barcelona. He was on the table next to us!*

VOCABULARY

Relationships

argue (with someone)
be kind (to someone)
be rude (to someone)
get angry (with someone)
get on well (with someone)
hang out (with someone)
look after (someone)
make (someone) laugh
say sorry (to someone)
shout (at someone)

Kind acts

give
help
invite
offer
pick up litter
raise money
smile
thank

SPEAKING

Persuading

Do you fancy ... with me?
Come on, it'll be fun!
We really should do it.
Think of ...
I'm not sure.
I'll think about it.
I suppose so.
You've persuaded me!

WRITING

Describing someone you know well

We've known each other for ...
We've been friends since ...
We met when ...
I like him/her because ...
He/She's into ...
We've got a lot in common, for example ...

Adjective order

Martha's got **long dark** hair.
She's got **beautiful brown** eyes.

LANGUAGE SUMMARY

UNIT 9

GRAMMAR

used to

Affirmative	Negative
I/You/She/He/We/They **used to live** in Poland.	I/You/She/He/We/They **didn't use to like** cheese.
Questions	**Short answers**
Did you **use to play** tennis?	Yes, I **did**. / No, I **didn't**.
Did they **use to have** a dog?	Yes, they **did**. / No, they **didn't**.

Rules

We use *used to* to talk about actions that happened regularly in the past. We use *used to* for things that were true in the past, but aren't true now.

The negative form of *used to* is *didn't use to* (not *didn't used to*).

have to and *don't have to*, *must* and *mustn't*

Affirmative	
I/You/We/They **have to wear** a uniform.	
He/She **has to help** with the cooking.	
I/You/He/She/We/They **must pay attention** in class.	
Negative	
I/You/We/They **don't have to dress** smartly.	
He/She **doesn't have to do** much homework.	
I/You/He/She/We/They **mustn't drop** litter.	
Questions	**Short answers**
Do you **have to tidy** your room?	Yes, I **do**. / No, I **don't**.
Does she **have to cook** lunch?	Yes, she **does**. / No, she **doesn't**.

Rules

We use *have to* to say that something is necessary.

Have to has a similar meaning to *must*.

Don't have to and *mustn't* have completely different meanings.

We use *don't have to* to say that something is not necessary (but you can do it if you want to).

We use *mustn't* to say that something is not permitted.

Indefinite pronouns

	Person	Place	Thing
Affirmative	someone/somebody	somewhere	something
Negative / Questions	anyone/anybody	anywhere	anything

Rules

We use indefinite pronouns to refer to people, places and things when we don't say exactly who, where or what we are talking about.

We use pronouns starting with *some-* for affirmative sentences and pronouns starting with *any-* for negative sentences and questions.

VOCABULARY

Life stages

Adjectives	Nouns
elderly	adult
grown-up	newborn baby
married	teenager
middle-aged	toddler
retired	young adult

Talking about age

She's in her twenties.
He's in his fifties.

School rules

arrive on time
chew gum
dress smartly
drop litter
follow instructions
forget your books
keep your classroom tidy
pay attention
put your hand up
run in the corridors
use bad language
don't wear jewellery

SPEAKING

Talking about rules

You have to …
You don't have to …
We all have to …
You aren't allowed to …
Is it OK to …?

WRITING

Giving information

You should …
I suggest that you …
You won't need …
You have to / don't have to …

Opinion adverbs

Unfortunately, it usually rains a lot in November.
Luckily, exchange students don't have to wear a uniform!

IRREGULAR VERBS LIST

Infinitive		Past simple		Past participle	
be	/bi/	was/were	/wəz, wɒz, wə(r), wɜː(r)/	been	/bɪn, biːn/
become	/bɪˈkʌm/	became	/bɪˈkeɪm/	become	/bɪˈkʌm/
begin	/bɪˈgɪn/	began	/bɪˈgæn/	begun	/bɪˈgʌn/
break	/breɪk/	broke	/brəʊk/	broken	/ˈbrəʊkən/
bring	/brɪŋ/	brought	/brɔːt/	brought	/brɔːt/
build	/bɪld/	built	/bɪlt/	built	/bɪlt/
buy	/baɪ/	bought	/bɔːt/	bought	/bɔːt/
can	/kən, kæn/	could	/kəd, kʊd/		
come	/kʌm/	came	/keɪm/	come	/kʌm/
cost	/kɒst/	cost	/kɒst/	cost	/kɒst/
do	/də, du/	did	/dɪd/	done	/dʌn/
draw	/drɔː/	drew	/druː/	drawn	/drɔːn/
drink	/drɪŋk/	drank	/dræŋk/	drunk	/drʌŋk/
drive	/draɪv/	drove	/drəʊv/	driven	/ˈdrɪvn/
eat	/iːt/	ate	/eɪt, et/	eaten	/ˈiːtn/
fall	/fɔːl/	fell	/fel/	fallen	/ˈfɔːlən/
feel	/fiːl/	felt	/felt/	felt	/felt/
find	/faɪnd/	found	/faʊnd/	found	/faʊnd/
fly	/flaɪ/	flew	/fluː/	flown	/fləʊn/
get	/get/	got	/gɒt/	got	/gɒt/
give	/gɪv/	gave	/geɪv/	given	/ˈgɪvn/
go	/gəʊ/	went	/went/	gone/been	/gɒn, biːn/
have	/həv, hæv/	had	/hæd/	had	/hæd/
hear	/hɪə(r)/	heard	/hɜːd/	heard	/hɜːd/
know	/nəʊ/	knew	/njuː/	known	/nəʊn/
learn	/lɜːn/	learnt/learned	/lɜːnt, lɜːnd/	learnt/learned	/lɜːnt, lɜːnd/
leave	/liːv/	left	/left/	left	/left/
lose	/luːz/	lost	/lɒst/	lost	/lɒst/
make	/meɪk/	made	/meɪd/	made	/meɪd/
meet	/miːt/	met	/met/	met	/met/
put	/pʊt/	put	/pʊt/	put	/pʊt/
read	/riːd/	read	/red/	read	/red/
ride	/raɪd/	rode	/rəʊd/	ridden	/ˈrɪdn/
run	/rʌn/	ran	/ræn/	run	/rʌn/
say	/seɪ/	said	/sed/	said	/sed/
see	/siː/	saw	/sɔː/	seen	/siːn/
sell	/sel/	sold	/səʊld/	sold	/səʊld/
send	/send/	sent	/sent/	sent	/sent/
sing	/sɪŋ/	sang	/sæŋ/	sung	/sʌŋ/
sleep	/sliːp/	slept	/slept/	slept	/slept/
speak	/spiːk/	spoke	/spəʊk/	spoken	/ˈspəʊkən/
stand	/stænd/	stood	/stʊd/	stood	/stʊd/
swim	/swɪm/	swam	/swæm/	swum	/swʌm/
take	/teɪk/	took	/tʊk/	taken	/ˈteɪkən/
teach	/tiːtʃ/	taught	/tɔːt/	taught	/tɔːt/
tell	/tel/	told	/təʊld/	told	/təʊld/
think	/θɪŋk/	thought	/θɔːt/	thought	/θɔːt/
throw	/θrəʊ/	threw	/θruː/	thrown	/θrəʊn/
wear	/weə(r)/	wore	/wɔː(r)/	worn	/wɔːn/
win	/wɪn/	won	/wʌn/	won	/wʌn/
write	/raɪt/	wrote	/rəʊt/	written	/ˈrɪtn/